"Jason Wright sets out a practical
inspire managers to create a winnin

Olympic Performance Director at th. ...on

"Jason has not only raised his own ga. .at of everyone else around him, and the lessons on h. .v to achieve this are captured here for us to share."

Jeremy Snape,
Performance Coach to the SA Cricket Team, and
former International Cricketer

"Jason is passionate and practical – a combination that works extremely well in this book – giving readers some concrete ways to engage and motivate their teams as well as overcome the typical obstacles that managers face. Good quality, honest conversations are at the heart of this book – with positive results."

Angela McHale,
Director, Steps Drama Learning Development

"Jason is a practitioner not a theorist – his practical and enthusiastic approach to leadership is captured well in this book making it the ideal guide for other managers to use to lead their teams and deliver sustainable results."

Lyn Etherington,
Co-author of 'Customer Loyalty – A Guide for Time Travellers' and
Director of Cape Consulting Ltd

"I have always believed that developing and coaching people through individual productive relationships is the best way to improve their performance. *Making Sense of Performance Management* clearly shows how a strong people culture with emphasis on continuous improvement will deliver superior results."

Alan Rapley,
GB Olympic Swimming Captain and
Director of Alan Rapley Consultancy Ltd

For a complete list of Management Books 2000 titles
visit our web-site on http://www.mb2000.com

MAKING SENSE OF PERFORMANCE MANAGEMENT

Jason Wright

Jay,

All the best with your performance journey - keep Spiralling!

Jason

2000

First published in 2010 by Management Books 2000 Ltd
Forge House, Limes Road
Kemble, Cirencester
Gloucestershire, GL7 6AD, UK
Tel: 0044 (0) 1285 771441
Fax: 0044 (0) 1285 771055
Email: info@mb2000.com
Web: www.mb2000.com

British Library Cataloguing in Publication Data is available

ISBN 9781852526306

Acknowledgements

Thanks to everyone who has encouraged me to write this book, and to everyone who has inspired the material in it by being "on the journey" with me.

Thanks to Jeremy Snape, for his personal contribution to the book; and to Nick Dale-Harris, for his advice and ideas throughout its development and production.

Special thanks to my wife Karen to whom I am indebted for her unconditional support. She has been by my side every step of the way, and along with our daughters Hannah and Jennifer, my source of inspiration throughout.

Jason Wright
www.performancespiral.co.uk

To Karen.

For your love, friendship, patience and encouragement.

Contents

Foreword

I expect that it is only people who are very keen to improve their performance who will be reading this book. The problem with this is that I have been given the dubious honour of writing the first words you will read! "What does a former professional cricketer know about performance management in business?" I hear you cry. Well, I asked myself that question too at one stage, but as I became more integrated into business performance I could see huge parallels with my former career.

Having played 19 years as a professional and represented England 11 times in International One Day cricket I have had my own varied experiences of performance. Lots of setbacks and challenges interspersed with days of great success both as a player and as a county captain. I have played in teams full of stars who failed to reach their goals, and also with teams of lesser names who filled trophy cabinets year after year. Throughout my personal journey, I became fascinated with what it was that made some players good and others great when there was no discernable difference in talent.

This fascination led me to study an MSc in sport psychology at Loughborough University before I retired from cricket to embark on a career in performance coaching for both sport and business. After forming the performance consultancy *Sporting Edge* I have witnessed a huge upturn in the demand for performance coaching, and a growing synergy between top class sporting teams and their counterparts in business. Currently I am working with the South African national Cricket Team as they strive to reach world 'number one' status in all forms of the game, Shane

Warne's Rajasthan Royals in the Indian Premier League, and various corporate clients in the UK and abroad – each one faces different challenges, but share the common theme of striving for performance excellence.

Never before has our personal performance been so transparent under the scrutiny of Key Performance Indicators and a constant barrage of appraisals and target reviews which mirror the replays and slow motion technical dissections from every angle in sport. Add to this the exponential spread of media and internet information, and within a matter of seconds not only have we had our own performance measured but everyone across the world can see it! Whether in sport or business, this transparency and speed of communication has undoubtedly added to our lives, but it has also brought more potential stress from the constant stream of Blackberries bleeping, Facebooks flickering and Twitters twittering.

If our coping skills don't keep pace with these burgeoning pressures then we could face an overburdening future. 'Psychobabble' isn't enough either. It's not just about being positive – it's about being real. Often the best tips are common sense but they need to be integrated into our habits to become common practice. The book which you are holding gives you that opportunity.

For those students of performance who are used to the endless shelves of self-help books, you may be disappointed. There will be no philosophical quotes here, just real life examples of what we all face day in, day out. *Making Sense of Performance Management* offers not only pages of practical advice but a clear view of the tangible skills which any top manager can use to take their team closer to their potential. The motivational talks from sporting icons or Arctic explorers, like many academic theories, are very interesting – but it is the accessibility of this particular performance journey which makes it a compelling read.

Whether we work with a ball or a ballpoint, it seems that with increased pressure we all tend to doubt our ability, so we try to do something special. This book will offer lessons that the special thing is actually to understand yourself and deliver your own basic game more brilliantly than before. No flashy concepts just better basics which will make us more effective.

The high-performing team is in a constant state of dynamism with people competing externally and internally for the spoils of success. My experience of playing and working with these teams suggests that the culture of the organisation plays a huge role in determining what these spoils should be. Despite the outside world craving number one rankings and financial bonuses, these things are only achieved when our processes are functioning efficiently. Coaching this concept has been a common thread of my work whether I am working with Graeme Smith's South African Team in their whites, or Jason Wright's leadership group in their suits. This book shows not only why process wins over outcome every time, but actually how this is achieved in developing and maintaining a high-performance culture along the turbulent journey.

Our daily habits and schedules actually reflect our personal choices and having an objective check on these can often be very refreshing. Whereas sportsmen practise more than they play, the business world can simulate this in planning and using effective routines and models to remain focused, rather than just turning up and doing what we have always done from 8.59am to 5.01pm. Jason highlights how these practice habits can support you in high pressure situations.

The common theme throughout this book is how a high-performance culture is actually crafted through the strong yet subtle management of people. Having worked with Jason over the last few years I have seen the respect which he has earned from his team. With more success has come a bigger team for him, but rather than keep the safe mentality he has embraced his new challenges, and found a way to bring the team up to his level of expectation time after time. Jason has not only raised his own game but that of everyone else around him, and the lessons on how to achieve this are captured here for us to share.

Quality leaders have a clear vision of where they are going, a genuine care for their 'players', and a passion which fuels everyone's desire to overcome the barrage of challenges and reach the top. In sport and in business we are not looking for the player who can be 'good on their day'. We need to lead people in such a way that they will strive 365 days every year for high performance. A winning mindset is critical to our success in this, and, in our approach to sustained learning towards future successes. I hope that you enjoy *Making Sense of Performance Management* as it assists you to achieve peak performance.

Jeremy Snape
Performance Coach to the SA Cricket Team
www.thesportingedge.co.uk

1

Beginning Our High-Performance Journey

Performance has become part of everyday life.

Twenty four hours a day, seven days a week, news broadcasts report on global political and economic performance. Analysts and journalists scrutinise everything from the world's stock markets to locally provided public services. In business the performance of major companies is examined, as is the performance of high profile individuals. In sport, television coverage highlights every possible performance statistic available, before, during, and after the event. In entertainment, critics provide us with regular reviews on the best and worst performances in recent shows, films, concerts and other productions. Clearly, performance is of great importance.

Knowing this, manufacturers spend huge sums of money telling us *their* product performs better. Whether it is batteries that last longer, razors that shave closer, washing powders that get our whites even whiter, or bleach that kills more germs than ever before, they believe we will want to buy a product that performs better. They are right, because good performance impresses us. Many of the big decisions we make in life are based on the pursuit of superior performance. For example, we may be prepared to move house so that our children can attend a school that has a strong performance track record. We may pay for advice on where to invest our money in the hope that we will get a better performance return. We may choose to take a job with a different company because we want to work in a business that performs better. All of these are big decisions that are influenced by our view of other people's performance.

It shouldn't come as a surprise then to find that our own performance is under scrutiny too. Experts claim that by following their advice we can enhance our physical and mental performance. We are regularly faced with questions about our lifestyle. Do we take enough exercise? Do we drink enough water? Do we eat a balanced diet?

However, for us personally, the most significant area where our performance really matters is in the way we make a living. At every level, every role in every business requires specific performance standards to be met and it would be easy to assume that these performance standards are set for us. In reality though, each and every one of us chooses our own performance benchmark. Whether we set our benchmark high or low is our own choice. Our first challenge is to make that choice a conscious decision. Many people believe that high performance and the success it brings is a gift reserved for the 'lucky few' who are born with unique qualities and personality traits. This may sound like a cop-out, but there is a good reason why there are many who share this view. Individuals with charisma, flair and high levels of natural ability often make success look easy. If we assume that their success comes from the abilities they were born with, and also conclude that *we* were not gifted with similar innate ability, then it's easy to form the opinion that high performance is a gift, rather than a reward for hard work. As a result of this thought process many people conclude that high levels of achievement are beyond their grasp and so they set their personal benchmark lower. In fact, very few successful people were simply 'born like that'. However easy it may look, successful people work hard to deliver the results that we measure their performance by. They will probably have had to take some calculated risks, and make brave decisions along the way. In essence, however easy it may appear, success doesn't come easily. It requires effort.

We should find this reassuring because it means that the level of success we ultimately achieve is entirely our own choice. Success is freely available to all of us. We just need to make it a conscious decision to work hard towards a successful outcome, whatever that outcome is for us personally.

That decision is just the start of the journey. For our journey to progress we have to learn how to evaluate and manage our performance along the way. Whether it is on an individual level or as a team, making sense of how to manage performance is critical to our success. We need to develop our performance management capability so that we can inspire those we lead to raise their personal benchmark and deliver a bigger performance.

On the face of it there is a lot of help available to us. There are countless theories and models, an abundance of case studies and research, and shelves full of management books and business manuals. This can become very confusing. After all we often find ourselves in a management or leadership position by virtue of the fact that we have been successful in our previous role and we earn a promotion as a result. Alternatively we may have set up a small business that has expanded and instead of simply managing ourselves we suddenly find that we have responsibility for managing others! In either case it is probably true to say that our success to date hasn't been based purely on theory, models or the contents of a book. More often than not it will have been based on our own personal ability and our individual skill coupled with our passion to do a great job. Moving into management and making sense of how we manage the performance of others may not come as naturally. We may find that we are not able to rely on the intuitive approach that has served us so well previously. If we are serious about becoming great performance managers then it is essential that we learn how to develop effective management and leadership skills to the point where they too become intuitive and instinctive. Achieving this by trying to unravel theory is something that many managers find difficult to do. What we really need is practical common sense guidance on how to develop a style of performance management that drives superior results.

> - How can we make sense of performance management?
>
> - Is there a simple, straightforward formula for success?
>
> - What are the lessons that we can learn through the experiences of others?
>
> - How can we translate our own experiences into sound management and leadership practice?

Many new managers fall into the trap of trying to deliver a stereotype, acting in a way they think they ought to behave. Perhaps they feel that simply being themselves may not be enough to get them through the most difficult career transition they are likely to make. So they try to emulate someone else's style, or attempt to become the type of manager they think is expected. Maybe the reason for this is that they don't have a framework to base their own management style around that they can confidently rely upon to make them successful.

Identifying such a framework, and then continually developing the skills of the managers I worked with, became a passion for me. I wanted them to feel that being a part of my team was like being on a journey to high performance. That journey would have its challenges and there would, at times, be bumps and bends in the road. However the milestones that we would pass along the way would provide reassurance that we were on track to reach our high-performance destination. I have often described this journey as a non-stop rollercoaster of development – full of ups and downs, but always an exciting ride! Throughout such a dynamic journey many important lessons are learned which, along with the experiences, anecdotes and stories that are gathered along the way, aids our progress towards achieving a high-performance goal. I found that it was these lessons, and the stories that brought them to life, that made sense to people, by helping them to apply practical straightforward ideas for success that they could relate to and refer back to. This was not just about theories that might work – it became a formula for success that could be used every day.

In contrast, most of the stories told in performance-related books are about *high-profile* success – in sports they might feature national teams winning a world cup or a prestigious trophy – or individuals who have won a major tournament or an Olympic medal. In business they feature the successes of well-known CEOs, or entrepreneurs who have made millions. My experience is much more down to earth, but no less significant to the people I have worked closely with, because many of these everyday people in everyday jobs didn't find it easy to relate to the experiences of the rich and famous. Their roles and their goals were also much more down to earth, but that did not mean that they had any less desire to be successful. They wanted to work in an environment where they were understood, where they could raise their issues openly and without fear, be provided with support to overcome their challenges, and receive sufficient development to enable them to achieve the level of success they personally aspired to.

Like many other people, I have been influenced over the years by the views, theories, and models of prominent business 'thinkers', as well as the experiences and achievements of well-known sports stars and successful business people. However I have probably been influenced more by the practical experiences I have learned from simply by being there, right in the thick of it, day after day. Reflecting on this made me realise that making sense of performance management requires neither complex theory, nor exceptional natural talent. It is simply all about making sense of the everyday activities that, if delivered in the right way, at the right time, to the right people, will lead to a superior performance – which is something that all performance managers want to achieve.

Over a number of years I have enjoyed leading and managing people in different sized teams, some as small as five or six, others several hundred strong, and in every role I have always strived to deliver a brand of leadership that is practical and based on common sense. There is no doubt that people respond positively to a straightforward, uncluttered and concise approach that they can easily understand and relate to. My experiences throughout this time shaped my leadership style, and influenced the way I developed relationships with those I worked with. I have often been encouraged to share these experiences with others, which is precisely what this book does, by helping to make sense of performance management through developing a practical, reliable framework that we can combine with our personal skills, abilities, ideas and ambitions, to lead our team on a journey to high performance.

So how do we begin to make sense of performance management? We start by recognising that businesses and teams are, by nature, dynamic. They cannot be static, so if they are not moving forwards, they will be moving backwards. I have often illustrated this by using the image of a spiral and asking whether the spiral is going upwards or downwards. This is a difficult question to answer unless we can actually see the movement. If we want to make sense of performance management we must be aware of everything that can influence the speed or direction of our performance spiral, and accept that it is our challenge to manage the movement in an upward direction. As we begin to make sense of the key drivers within the performance management framework and understand how we can influence the impact they have on performance, we will be able to maintain upward momentum and we will reap the benefits.

In any performance-measured role it will always be the outputs or the results that we are ultimately judged on. We accept that this will be the case as one way or another it is the results that pay our wages. However being focused on outputs alone can mean that we don't place enough emphasis on the inputs. This could cause us to become distracted from the things that really matter. For example, even though it sounds ridiculous, we could easily forget the importance of creating a happy and motivated workforce. Pressure situations can distract us very quickly and we may even fail to remember that it is the individuals in our team who deliver the results for us, and without them we wouldn't have any outputs or results to measure.

How can we avoid falling into this trap? To answer this question we must begin by recognising that successful performance management stems from the culture we create for our team, and our culture is built more on inputs than on outputs. Simply put, if we develop a winning culture then higher levels of performance will follow. If we are serious about becoming world class performance managers we need to be serious about building a culture that works to deliver all the aspects of our business scorecard in the right proportions at the right times and with the right result.

Many performance management techniques have too narrow a focus. Often I have seen managers pushing one area really hard, only to find that they have done so at the expense of another.

Inevitably they receive a reminder that it is their job to 'keep all the plates spinning'! In response to this 'encouragement' their focus switches to the area that had been detrimentally affected, but this only results in the same outcome. It is easy to get stuck in this cycle by continually setting short-term targets and delivering short-term results. This approach is very short-sighted and will only ever produce non-sustainable results, which is why the cycle keeps repeating. Unfortunately this transactional style of management has become commonplace. There has to be a better way, though – we need something built to last, not just built to be fast.

Perhaps the first thing to learn and accept is that there are no real quick fixes. Nevertheless, even though a high-performance culture cannot be created overnight, we must still act quickly and decisively to begin working towards that goal. We can begin by developing a clear framework which we can build on by adding a programme of ongoing activities that will continually shape, expand, and enhance our high-performance culture.

That framework is based on the four key areas that will have an enormous influence upon the culture we create for our team, as illustrated in the diagram overleaf. We will explore each of these in turn in the sections that follow.

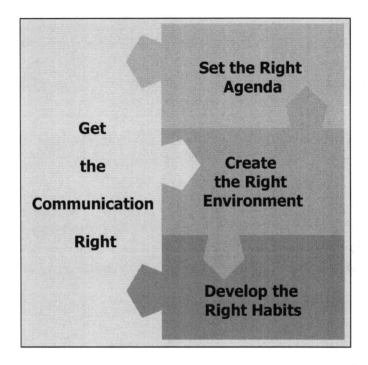

By developing the practical aspects of leadership that are required to underpin these four areas we will be able to make sense of performance management. We will increase our understanding of the importance of people engagement within our team, and how we can drive higher engagement levels to strengthen our team culture. We will see that our role as a performance manager is central to the culture we create, and the more we influence high quality inputs the more confident we can be that our team will deliver high performance outputs.

It is important that we have some fun along the way too. After all, we spend many hours at work, and so do those who work along with us. If our development journey is like a rollercoaster ride it will be fun and exciting most of the time, but the twists and turns may also make it a little frightening. We should always remember the importance of keeping people happy and engaged so they have a smile on their faces even during challenging times. If people continue to have fun and enjoy the ride we will begin to reap the rewards that high performance brings.

Having established a solid performance framework, and made a conscious decision to set off on a journey towards high performance, we can relax, be ourselves, and enjoy where our journey takes us.

2

Get the Communication Right

Tools and skills

We are all familiar with the everyday sayings, 'tools of the trade' and 'tricks of the trade'. Such phrases have originated because it is commonly accepted that the correct tools, and the right level of knowledge, must combine for someone to be effective and efficient in their job. We are also familiar with the phrase, 'a bad worker blames his tools!' This expression highlights the fact that skill is needed as well, because the correct tools are only of benefit if they are used by someone who knows how to do so skilfully.

In most professions or trades, it is easy to identify the tools and skills that are required in order to do that particular job well. For example, if we imagine a plumber, or a joiner, we probably find that tools such as spanners and saws immediately spring to mind. If we think of a doctor, or a dentist, we probably quickly conjure up images of a white coat and a stethoscope, or a reclining chair and a drill. So we have a mental image of the tools that these people use, and to complete the picture we naturally begin to think about the skills we expect them to display as well. This will be especially true if we intend to employ them personally, to undertake maintenance or repairs in our home or to look after our health. Under these circumstances we will be very quick to identify the level of skill we require of them. The reason we do this is that we feel the need to make a performance assessment. In so doing, we judge the individuals engaged in such professions or trades on two things. Firstly do they possess the right tools for their trade? Secondly, do they exhibit the right skill level to do a good quality job? Based on the answers we arrive at, we make a performance assessment of the result they are likely to deliver for us.

What happens if we consider jobs like 'general manager', 'unit manager', 'section head', 'sales manager', 'team leader', 'centre manager', 'area manager', and 'regional manager'? The type of roles that, most likely, many readers of this book will be employed in. When we tell others about our role as a people manager or performance manager, what do they visualise? Can they readily identify the tools *we* use or the skills *we* possess, in the same way as they would do for a plumber, a joiner, a doctor or a dentist? In truth they find it much more difficult, so they tend to ask different questions such as, "what does your company do?" or "what does your team do?" What is interesting about this, is that people still want to make a performance assessment, but rather than basing their assessment on the tools and the skills we use personally in our day-to-day role, they use the outcome, or result, we are employed to deliver as their reference point. This could be because great management techniques are not easy to recognise and assess, or it could be that people management is not universally viewed as a profession that requires effective tools and demands great skill. Perceptions like these are actually quite dangerous for us, because we can be tricked into believing that it is only the result that matters and not the way we go about delivering it.

There is an interesting debate around whether management should be regarded as a profession or not. However it is not the status of the role that we should be most interested in defining, it is our attitude towards it. All of us would accept that there are big differences between established professions such as law and medicine on the one hand, and everyday people management on the other. Even so, everyone would agree that managers and leaders should act in a professional way, so it is reasonable to expect that performance managers should be judged on the way they carry out their 'profession' or 'trade', as well as on the results and outcomes they deliver. If we look at it this way, then we quickly realise that if we want to be truly effective performance managers we have to focus on the tools and skills we employ – the way in which we do our job – and not just the end results we achieve.

All of which begs the question – how should we assess the performance of a performance manager? And, if our assessment suggests that we have room for improvement, how can we develop ourselves to reach the right standard?

Our answer centres on a number of key disciplines that a skilled performance manager will need to be highly proficient in. Throughout this book we will explore in detail the tools and the skills that we must acquire and develop. However before we go any further, it is important to recognise that there is a central, core skill, without which it is impossible for us to be an effective performance manager. That skill is communication.

The central skill

Let's think about some of the tools we use that will test our communication skill. For example, when we are chairing a meeting, delivering a presentation, offering feedback, holding a coaching session, or conducting a one-to-one performance review, the core skill we employ is communication. All these events are our 'tools of the trade' – but the better our communication *skill* is, the more effective we will be in using these tools, and ultimately we will yield better results from each of these management activities. Therefore, when planning our development as a performance manger it is a good idea to place greater focus on improving this core skill of communication. The reason for this is simple. Communication is really the 'glue' that holds all the other aspects of performance management together. It is central to everything we do. That being the case, developing really strong communication skills is essential for us. Very few managers would claim to be natural, charismatic, leaders who get everything right all of the time, without using some sort of blueprint or model to base their management style on. Whilst pure theory is not necessarily what we are looking for here, it is true to say that a solid and reliable framework will give us a distinct advantage as we learn how to become better communicators.

Quite early in my first role involving leadership of other managers, it became necessary to recruit a new manager to head up the largest unit in my business area. I set about preparing the questions that I would ask the candidates at interview. I wanted to design a set of questions that would help me to select the right manager for that specific unit, but also would identify an individual who would complement the overall management team. One of the questions that I posed in those interviews has stayed with me ever since. It was, "I believe that communication is the lifeblood of successful leadership. How will you convince me that you have the necessary communication skills to succeed in this role?" The answers to the question helped me to recruit a really strong communicator. However that is not the reason why this question has stayed with me for many years – it has done so because I ask it repeatedly of both myself, and others. Analysing the answers and applying the learning, has had a significant influence on my own management style and on the approach I have taken when coaching others to develop better communication skills. Asking a candidate at interview "How will you convince me you have the necessary communication skills?" is a good start. However understanding how to answer that question each and every day is the real key. For anyone who aspires to be a great performance manager it is a question that needs to be asked regularly because communication really is the central skill in performance management and successful leadership.

A vital part of our role as a performance manager involves taking responsibility for providing the knowledge, skills, direction, and motivation needed by our team. This is not something we do once and then sit back to await the results. Our responsibility extends to seeking and gathering feedback that will support the ongoing development and growth of the people in our team. All of this must be achieved through effective communication. If we analyse what is required here we may quickly realise that this is actually a very tall order. On that basis we could ask, "Is it possible to teach managers to be great communicators, or is it necessary to recruit people who are already great communicators?" We might conclude that because communication is a skill then surely, just like any other skill, it can be taught or coached. On the other hand, we may feel that it would be much easier if we could simply recruit the best communicators available to us. In truth, both effective development of our existing team, *and* recruitment of the right people in future, will play a critical role in our success. However we must also focus on our own development as leaders – getting our communication right involves a great deal more.

As we have already acknowledged, successful performance management has its roots in the culture established by the leader. This means that to deliver a high-performance goal the importance of getting our communication right takes on an even greater significance. It involves setting the required tone, and then 'regulating the temperature' of our team environment. It is vitally important that we take personal responsibility for leading this, because if *we* don't, someone else will. Others will happily assume control of the tone, or 'temperature', in a team if it becomes evident that the leader is not doing so. This happens because the communication flow will continue whether we are in control of it or not. This presents us with a very different risk to be aware of, and to mitigate. For example, if as a leader we don't do any coaching it is unlikely that anyone else in the team will fill the void – there would simply be an absence of coaching. If we don't tackle issues such as lateness or attendance, our team won't fix those issues for us, they will just test the boundaries to see how much they can get away with. Communication is very different because a group of people will not allow a void to develop. Our team will not attempt to find out how long they can cope without communication. No, they will gladly fill that gap for us, and when they do so *they* begin to regulate the team environment instead of us. Communication is sure to exist, but it may not be the type of communication that is most beneficial for our team, or that best supports a high-performance culture.

At this point it is important to recognise that the communication flow in our business will either be healthy or detrimental. There is no middle ground. Therefore, a big part of our role as a performance manager involves proactively taking responsibility for managing the communication in our team to avoid the risks that could arise if someone else assumes responsibility, either deliberately, or by default. That way we remain in control of a powerful asset instead of accruing a dangerous liability. I have always referred to this as 'regulating the temperature', and learning how to do this effectively is one of the essential ingredients for creating a high-performing team.

Regulating the temperature

To explain this we can briefly refer back to the example of the interview question about communication being the lifeblood of successful leadership. Within the answer given by the candidates I was expecting them to be able to demonstrate that they knew how to communicate to inspire, motivate, coach, lead and direct. I knew that if they were able to do this successfully, they would effectively set a 'temperature' in their team that was conducive to success. It is easy to have a short-term impact as a new manager, but if we want to enjoy longer-term success we must develop the ability to regulate the 'temperature' in our team on an ongoing basis.

A leader needs to exercise control without being controlling. The phrase 'regulating the temperature' may sound very controlling, but it isn't really. It's less about being in control of every action, and more about being in control of the overall outcome. By regulating the 'temperature' in our business we can influence the right outcomes without having a direct hand in all the activities that will take place to deliver that outcome. Mastering the art of being in control without behaving in a controlling manner is essential to making sense of performance management.

We should recognise that many people tend to approach their role in a transactional way rather than a strategic way. In other words, they deliver each aspect of their role as separate transactions and may not find it easy to see the bigger picture without our support. For example they could view Monday's meeting on revenues as a separate transaction from Tuesday's session on marketing and Wednesday's discussion on customer service. However, in reality all these meetings may have been convened under the theme *"How to Satisfy our Customers' Needs Profitably"*. Recognising that this same tendency will probably exist in our team, we should endeavour to counteract it by developing a cultural management style rather than adopting a transactional approach in our leadership.

To explain this more fully consider the following example. I remember talking with a department head about a time when external market pressures had dictated a change in focus for his team. The managers in the unit had provided assurances that they knew what was required and that they had enough ideas and expertise to succeed. After a short period of time they realised that were not as well equipped for the challenge as they had originally thought, so they returned to ask for more ideas. The department head promptly furnished them with a list of activities that were known to have worked in a different business, along with some of his own ideas that he knew, from past experience, would work under the circumstances. Later still, it transpired that these ideas had not been implemented properly, and performance continued to suffer. The management team were frustrated and the department head equally so.

When we analysed what had happened we came to the conclusion that the outcome would have been significantly better had a cultural management style been more evident. What had actually taken place, probably due to the pressure of the situation and the need for a swift solution, was transactional. Simply put, a request for ideas was met with the provision of a list of ideas. The request was satisfied by way of a transaction, whereas in reality the management team needed to be engaged in the solution so that they could buy into the ideas they generated as a team, fully understand what was required, and then deliver a more successful outcome. If they had been brought together to work this through, the team would have been strengthened culturally at a time when they really needed to be operating closely together and relying on each other to increase the likelihood that they would succeed under pressure. Adopting this cultural management approach would have yielded a more positive end result.

Many business situations demand a speed of response that may lead to swift decisions and prompt implementation of solutions. At times we may feel we have little choice, and a quick reaction is our only alternative. However we should always consider whether this approach offers the best longer-term prospects. There are occasions when we need to be brave. Managing challenging situations using a cultural style may restrict the speed at which we are able to implement actions, but once mobilised the solutions we have generated will be much stronger because our team are fully engaged in delivering the agreed plan. Ultimately, we will achieve a positive result more quickly that also possesses better prospects for enduring success. By leading people in a cultural way we allow our team to control the actions whilst we remain in control of the outcome. This approach will effectively regulate a high-performance 'temperature' in our business.

By looking closely at the behaviours within our team we will always be able to see an indication of the current 'temperature' which will help us to determine appropriate leadership actions. I remember being told about a sales team who wanted to organise a party to celebrate a particularly impressive set of bonus payments that they had received. Initially the manager of the team thought that they were seeking some funding for the event, but it transpired that they simply wanted permission to organise the party and advertise it across the sales floor to get as many people involved as possible. The team had already agreed that they would pay for the party themselves out of their handsome bonuses! This was a great story because it said so much about the current 'temperature' in that department, and confirmed that the leadership team were regulating it well through a cultural management style. Without any control at all the sales team wouldn't have bothered to ask permission, they would have just done their own thing. With too much control they wouldn't have even raised the idea in the first place. Neither extreme is a good outcome. By regulating the 'temperature' in the right way though, we can open up a range of benefits which, as this example illustrates, includes releasing the creativity and initiative of the team around us. Often ideas generated from within a team are much more likely to hit the mark. This is a huge benefit because any group of managers, however good they are, cannot always come up with the best ideas themselves. Another benefit is that our team will be prepared to take ownership of making something happen that is important to them. This may not sound very significant upon first reading. However it is enormously significant compared to having people in our team who complain that nobody listens to them and who ultimately decide that there is no point asking for anything because their ideas are likely to be dismissed, or worse still ridiculed. In teams where the 'temperature' is regulated correctly the outcome will always be creative and positive.

Requests like this, which help us to gauge the 'temperature' in our team, do not always present themselves so directly. However, it is vital that we are always aware of the current 'temperature', so we must take steps to find out for ourselves. Accurate and timely feedback is absolutely essential, and we have to work out how we will obtain it. We can achieve this by building strong and reliable feedback loops, recognising that without them the cultural value of our communication will be lost.

I have often talked to managers about the difference between the 'boardroom' and the 'staffroom', asking them if they can be absolutely sure where the real power exists within their organisation. If a manager doesn't have a process for feedback that regulates the effectiveness of their communication, there is a risk that they could be undermined without realising it. If this continues then it is not possible to create a high-performance culture. For example, at the end of a presentation or meeting we have delivered, how do we know whether we have landed our message successfully or not? To answer this question we really need to know what is being said during the period of time immediately after the meeting ends. It is not unusual for people to leave a meeting and return to their desk via the coffee machine, water cooler, or rest rooms. The discussions that take place at this point will have a strong influence upon the way our message is received, and on the 'temperature' within our team. This is a really serious point, because these conversations will either reinforce or undermine the outcome we were aiming for.

Of course we must accept that, however well prepared a presentation or meeting is, there will invariably be a point of view that hasn't been considered. If that view is not uncovered and understood within the meeting, then it is sure to raise its head later on – more than likely when we are not present. This could spark more questions in the minds of those who attended the meeting which could cloud the message, or corrupt it altogether. If this were to happen, we would unknowingly lose control of the outcome, so it is imperative that we have appropriate feedback mechanisms in place to enable us to test and regulate both the 'temperature', and the communication flow in our team at all times.

It is not always feasible to simply ask for feedback at the end of a session and expect to receive it in the honest and constructive way that we need to hear it. A group will tend to conform, at least until they have had the opportunity to conduct a 'post-mortem' by the coffee machine! By the time this happens we are no longer managing the communication, and under these circumstances it is inevitable that the stronger ones in the group will influence others to their way of thinking. If these informal leaders are 'on side' they will support us, and we may still achieve a good outcome. However if they are not, then there is a risk that they will undermine us. Relying on such a process would be unwise because we have insufficient control over regulating the 'temperature'. If we are genuinely interested in testing the effectiveness of our communication to remain in control of the final successful outcome, we need to be savvy, and much more deliberate.

How can we achieve this? By capturing a process that we naturally follow many times in everyday life, and translating it into our business setting. As a general rule people like to hear an explanation of something before they experience it, then they will enjoy it and get more out of it. They will understand what to expect, enter into it more willingly, and be happy to talk about it honestly after the event. The process is as follows.

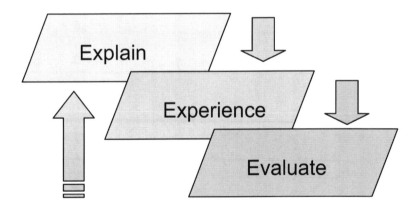

It is vital that we employ all three steps, in this order, to set the right 'temperature' in the first place, and then continue to regulate the 'temperature' afterwards. This will be a real benefit for our team, and will help us to acquire the honest feedback we need from them. The key lesson for us to learn here is that however effective an *experience* promises to be in isolation, it will be even more valuable if we have *explained* in advance of the event, and *evaluated* afterwards. Having accepted this fact it becomes important to develop really strong *explain* and *evaluate* techniques as part of our overall communication process. As well as building trust, and enabling us to motivate people to deliver the objectives we set for them, we will also be able to test and regulate the 'temperature' based on the feedback we get after their *experiences*. We can then repeat the cycle.

A thorough *explanation* is an effective way of linking forthcoming experiences to our core agenda so that people know precisely why that activity is important to them individually, or to the team they are a part of. How effective will any message be if people don't see how it links in to the bigger picture? Have you ever heard anyone say, "I really don't know why I was invited to that session" or "I don't know why I was sent on that course"? If we want the best performance outputs from the activities we plan, the meetings we run, or any other sessions we deliver, then we cannot leave anything to chance. We must *explain* clearly how each of these *experiences* contributes to the overall agenda and then demonstrate how that relates to those who are involved. All these *experiences*, large and small, are the building blocks of our business. Fitting them all together in a progressive and developmental way is key to driving success through creating a high-performance culture. As performance managers we must take this responsibility seriously.

There are many occasions where it is relevant to employ this process. For example, if a member of our team is due to attend a course we should meet up with them beforehand to *explain* why they are going, what we expect them to learn, how the content supports their personal development, and which aspects we want them to pay most attention to. It also makes sense to get their view on the reason for their attendance, and what benefits they anticipate the *experience* will offer them. After the event we should meet up again to *evaluate*. Were the aims met? Was the anticipated benefit received? How will any learning be implemented? If not, why not? What are the next steps we want to take?

We may think that this is fairly obvious for something as significant as a training course; however, many everyday situations arise where it is necessary to follow this process. For example we could even include something as simple as making a call to a client. Beforehand we can *explain* the importance of the call or the importance of that client to our business. We may remind the individual of recent coaching they have received that will help them to be more effective during the *experience*. We may also run through any barriers or challenges that could come up to help prepare for a successful outcome. Effective *evaluation* afterwards will afford us the opportunity to praise, offer further coaching, build confidence, or repair any damage.

By using the Explain, Experience, Evaluate process effectively, our everyday communication will consistently relate back to the strategic agenda to help our team to see the 'bigger picture' coming together clearly. This will support us in developing a cultural management style which drives high performance, rather than a transactional management style that simply gets the job done. We must always be thorough and specific when we *explain* to people why they need to be involved in an activity and what we expect them to get out of it. Then effective *evaluation* will ensure that the key messages have landed accurately, and the bigger picture is understood sufficiently well for people to talk about their *experiences* in a positive way.

I heard a very good example of this which occurred when a group of people were being trained on a new process that changed the way they input customer data into their computer system. Before they attended the course their manager *explained* why the training was necessary, what they would get out of it, and what the customer benefit was. All of this was accurately related back to the strategy of the unit. They found the course informative and beneficial and fit for purpose, so the *experience* was good for them too. However when they returned, the *evaluation* revealed that they didn't seem as enthusiastic about the new process as their manager thought they ought to have been. They were concerned that it would take them longer to input the data which would have a negative impact on their ability to meet their sales targets. This point of view had not been anticipated in the *explanation* or the *experience* because, in reality, the new process wouldn't take more time once they became used to it through practice. Clarifying this point in the *evaluation* stage meant that the end result was positive. This is a great example of how a leader needs to regulate the 'temperature' in their unit and can achieve a positive outcome by retaining control of the flow of communication without adopting a controlling style of management.

This instance also highlights the importance of following all three steps every time. Without each stage of the Explain, Experience, Evaluate process the outcome could have been very different. For a start the team may have conducted a coffee machine 'post mortem' and decided that the new process wasn't very good. As a result they could have become less motivated and performance may have slowed, but nobody in the leadership team would have known why. Hours and hours of management time could have become wrapped up in analysing the computer system and proposing expensive 'fixes' – when all that was needed was to follow the *evaluation* step of the process that costs nothing more than a little time!

Another example I recall which shows the importance of both the *explain* and *evaluate* stages, occurred when a team with a new manager was involved in a coaching session that was being facilitated by an external coach. This exact coaching session had been used to good effect previously, and the feedback had always been positive, so we were confident that the *experience* was good for the people who had been exposed to it. However on this occasion the *evaluation* revealed that the team thought the session was a waste of time. This didn't match up with other feedback we had received previously from other teams, so I asked their manager to help me understand fully how his team were feeling. It became clear quite early in our discussion that the *explain* stage had not been covered in enough depth. If the team had received a full *explanation* they would have known what to expect from the session and what it was designed to deliver for them. As a result their initial expectations and ultimate view on its value would probably have been different. This example reinforces the importance of using all three stages in the correct order to achieve the right outcome. It also highlights a second lesson, which is that sometimes the impact we achieve is very different to the impact we intended.

Impact versus intention

If our goal is to create a successful, high-performance culture, every aspect of our day-to-day communication needs to be precise and accurate to ensure that the impact of our communication is in tune with what we had intended. Unfortunately, this will not always be the case because communication is a two-way process that involves both a transmitter and a receiver, and at times either one, or both, of these could be faulty. It is important that we understand how the repercussions of this can be damaging to our high-performance culture.

I saw a good example of this in a team that was being managed by a newly appointed first-time manager. She wanted to get her team together socially to help them to bond as a team. This was a great idea that is commonly accepted as a good practice for any team at any time, but especially in those early stages of team development. She invited the team to join her on an evening out, but unfortunately only half the team were able to attend. Assuming that their reasons for not attending were genuine she arranged a second event, but the result was the same – only half the team got involved. After a few attempts to get the full team along to a social event, it became apparent that, instead of achieving her original intention of bonding the team closer together, this series of events had achieved the opposite impact. Rather than developing one team, two distinct groups had emerged. The first group was comprised of those who had been involved in the social events. They felt that the second group – those who hadn't joined in socially – were uninterested, disengaged, and had no desire to be part of the team. The situation needed to be resolved, and even though it was obvious to her that this impact was way off what she had initially intended the team manager still wanted to achieve her original aim. To her credit she sought to understand what the second group were thinking and how they were feeling. What she discovered was very revealing. The group who had never attended weren't excluding themselves because they didn't want to be part of the team; instead they had deliberately chosen not to get involved because they felt that they had been excluded from the decision-making process. Failing to consult with every member of the team meant that the planned social arrangements didn't fit with everyone's personal preferences. As is the case in many teams, this team was made up of different people with diverse backgrounds and differing family circumstances that restricted the types of event that some team members were able to get involved in. With hindsight this may sound obvious, but if more research had been done in advance the impact achieved would have been consistent with the original intention.

Despite not getting it right first time though, there was a

positive outcome in this instance because the manager challenged herself to get to the right result for her team. She wanted to identify a solution that would achieve her original intention of bringing them together. Having established much stronger communication, and a clear understanding of how to achieve the right outcome for everyone in the team, they started to do things differently. Firstly, whenever social events were arranged the team members themselves began to take the initiative to ensure the needs and preferences of the whole group were being considered. Secondly, it became possible for the day-to-day communication within the team to operate at a higher level, taking into account a broader range of opinions, views, ideas and solutions. This contributed to a high-performance culture which paid dividends. The team became a thoroughly bonded unit and their performance became much stronger. In fact, within a few months they were consistently one of the top performing teams in the unit. This outcome could have been very different if their manager had not learned how to manage impact versus intention at an early stage.

This example proves that when we are proactive we should always be absolutely clear from the start how we will successfully achieve our intended impact. The following example shows that, even if we choose to adopt a passive approach, we must still have total clarity of our intention. If we are not aware of all the possible impacts we carry a similar risk that we will not achieve our intended outcome.

A manager who was part of my leadership team at the time told me, "I can't keep working flat out like this, I'll give it another couple of weeks then I'll have to take my foot off the gas." He found himself simultaneously involved in three or four really important projects, and something was about to give. However he hadn't taken into account the fact that until his team were in a position to take ownership of the tasks that he was working 'flat out' to achieve, taking his 'foot off the gas' was not really a viable option. Doing so would be a mistake, and it would end in failure. Knowing that a passive approach was not really appropriate in this situation I asked him, "Have you told the team how you feel? They really need to know." Under the circumstances it was essential that his team take more ownership for delivery of the projects. Without clear communication though, there was no guarantee that they would do so. Obviously there was a risk that the impact the manager intended would not be achieved. We took the opportunity to plan the way forward to achieve a better outcome, one that would continue to get the job done but take the pressure off him. This included a clear communication plan that enabled him to set his team up in the right way, allowing him to safely move his focus and energy onto something else without putting his key projects in danger. Having an appropriate communication plan based on our desired outcome is the key. By starting with the desired outcome and working backwards, this manager changed his approach. Instead of thinking in a transactional way, which led him to the conclusion "I cannot keep working this hard", a sharper focus on the desired outcome helped him to think from a cultural standpoint, drawing the conclusion, "I need this tempo to continue, but I cannot keep running this fast personally". This correct thought process prompted a professional and mature planning discussion with his team, which clearly outlined the role each one of them needed to play to drive the business forward without exposing them to any risk. We can see from this experience how vital it is that we learn how to assess situations accurately, and then choose to communicate with our team in such a way that we achieve our intended impact. Thinking through the impacts and outcomes of the scenarios we face will help us to make the right choices in the way we communicate with our team. Before we deliver a message we should always prepare thoroughly, taking time to work through a full range of options and then deciding on the one most appropriate for each situation. Making sure that the impact we achieve matches the impact we intend needs to be a very deliberate process based around a clear desired outcome.

It is important to consider the audience. After all it is no consolation to claim after the event "Well, I knew what I meant"! However clear we think our communication is, it is of no use whatsoever if our audience doesn't understand our message. We may even cause serious damage if the impact of our message is not aligned to our original intention.

Answering the following questions may help us in our preparation.

- Why are we delivering this message?

- What is our desired outcome?

- What impact do we want to achieve?

- What are the risks?

- What are the potential 'blind spots'?

- What current circumstances or past experiences are worthy of consideration?

- What is the background of the audience?

- How well do we know them?

- Do we know what point of view they are likely to have?

- How can we acknowledge that we understand their point of view?

- What is the nature of our relationship with them?

- How can we create a benefit for them?

- What are they expecting us to say?

- Have we got sufficient credibility on the topic we are discussing?

- What do they need to hear to be motivated to change direction or change their behaviour?

- How do we intend to follow up?

The more thorough our preparation is, the more likely it is that we will plan our communication in such a way that we achieve our desired impact. We cannot leave anything to chance.

I once observed a team leader meeting taking place which illustrated this point well. One of the managers, who had some significant underperformance issues within his own team, was providing an update on two individuals in his team who were 'off the pace'. He was listing everything he had done to help them and all the reasons why their performance had not improved. He hadn't really prepared his message in advance, so it sounded more like a list of excuses than a summary of genuine reasons. However he received little or no challenge from the rest of the group. What was really going on here? Well this manager knew that his team performance wasn't good enough and he probably knew he hadn't done enough of the right things to fix it. So his *intention* was to 'survive' in front of his peers by coming up with the most plausible sounding explanations for the situation he was in. Based on the passive response he got from the rest of the group he could have been forgiven for believing that his desired *impact* had been achieved, but that was probably not the case. If we project forward we can speculate on what is likely to happen next. The manager who had made the excuses would walk away from the meeting with a sense of relief that he wasn't exposed to challenge. Then probably, albeit subconsciously, he may begin to work on what he will say next time he is in that position, rather than actually working on the problem itself so that he doesn't find himself in that situation again. The other managers may walk away thinking "he got away with it". Possibly there is a sense of relief that they had not been exposed to any challenge, or maybe they consider relaxing their own performance, thinking that they too could 'get away with' lower standards. Either way, it is very unlikely that they would be focused on how to solve the real problem by supporting their colleague towards improving his team's performance.

Having worked through this forward projection in my own mind I went to discuss my thoughts with the manager in question. I asked him how he felt the meeting had gone and what he had got out of it. I also asked him what he thought his colleagues may have gone away thinking about him. Most importantly though I asked him about the real issues in his team and what his long-term outcome needed to be. The answer became obvious to him – he needed to fix the performance problem. We then debated how setting up for 'survival' in a performance meeting was the wrong intended outcome. Instead, he should have approached the meeting with the long-term intention of fixing the problem in mind. This would have yielded a much more positive impact from his colleagues. For example, he could have asked for feedback on the current actions he had put in place and discussed alternative solutions to supplement his own ideas. He may have been able to identify what others were doing to address similar issues in their own teams. This approach would mean that he could have actually walked away from the meeting with a plan that made a real difference to the way he managed his team. The positive impact on the other managers must be noted too. They would have been stimulated towards thinking positively around solving a performance issue, working together as a team, and building confidence in their ability to find answers between them that could drive their collective performance spiral upwards.

Obviously there is a secondary lesson here for those who are responsible for chairing this type of meeting. We cannot allow the 'survival' instinct to get in the way of a *real* performance discussion. It is important to facilitate these sessions in such a way that the *impact* on our audience is beneficial and progressive. That way we will achieve our *intention* of improving team performance.

Taking the above example in a slightly different direction we can begin to explore the importance of our communication style when it comes to managing relationships. The manager involved hadn't realised that his actions in that meeting would either enhance or diminish the relationship he had with the other people sitting around that table which, in turn, would have a longer-term impact on his own performance contribution. To avoid any negative repercussions it is important to recognise that in relationship terms it is very difficult to achieve a neutral outcome. We will always have an impact on others when we come into contact with them and it is a fact of life that they will form an opinion of us – and surprisingly quickly. Their opinion may be fair and accurate or it may be completely wrong, but either way at that point in time that is their view of us. So the best outcome for us is that we always create a positive impact. We can achieve this by deciding precisely what our desired impact is and then rehearsing how we will achieve that consistently.

On the occasions when we communicate with a wider audience outside our normal working group, we need to be very deliberate in planning our impact and desired outcome with that specific audience in mind. It is likely that at least some members of the audience will not know us as well as our peers or subordinates do. That means that when they hear us speak they may not make the same allowances as people who know us better. It is essential then that we constantly challenge ourselves on the impact we create in these interactions, recognising that this very impact could cause people to form opinions about us that they hold for months, if not years, to come. Where our contact with people is less frequent we will be remembered and judged purely on what they see us do, and hear us say, in the few short interactions they observe, rather than what they would learn about us through a relationship that has been built up over time and is based on more frequent contact.

Ultimately we want to develop these interactions into relationships that will make a positive contribution to our own performance. Creating a great first impression is fundamental, but this is only the start. Moving forward from this point will test our skill in developing and managing relationships. How does this work? Simply put, a relationship is very similar to a bank account. Sometimes we pay in, other times we draw out. If our initial impact is positive then this could be considered the first deposit into the relationship account, but more work is needed as this process will only continue to work effectively as long as the relationship doesn't go 'overdrawn'.

Developing and managing relationships

It is not surprising that communication breakdown is listed second only to infidelity as a reason why couples divorce. It is obvious that it is impossible for one person to have a meaningful, lasting relationship with another in the absence of effective communication.

Equally, it is impossible to have a relationship with someone if we don't know anything about them. To have any level of relationship with another person we have to take a personal interest in them. We may talk to a neighbour about their neat garden, the alterations they have made to their house, or the new car that has appeared on their drive. We may talk to other parents at the school gate about school activities or the progress our children are making. We may talk to our local shopkeeper about current trade and how their business is doing. It sounds like these are just simple conversations, and they are just that if we do nothing more than have a friendly chat with these people every now and again. By taking more of a personal interest though, we create a desire in others to reciprocate and then a relationship begins to grow that both parties will be able to benefit from. For example, when the conversation with our neighbour results in us finding out exactly how they managed to get their grass to appear so lush, or the school gate conversation gives us some ideas on how to help our own child progress in an area they are struggling with, then a productive relationship develops. Our neighbour or fellow parent has enjoyed talking about something that is important to them because of the interest we have shown. In return we have found out something that we really wanted to know. The next time we meet, the relationship will deepen and the conversation will expand. For example, "Did you try that idea? Did it work? There's another thing you could try..."

In the everyday setting of the examples we have considered these may still appear to be general conversations, however if we translate this into our business environment we will discover a real benefit in performance terms. We cannot underestimate the value of this process. Developing and managing relationships is a huge contributor to our success.

Deliberately using such simple everyday examples to make the point proves that most people behave this way naturally in their day-to-day interactions with others without even realising it. By being conscious of such natural abilities, which are actually transferable skills, we can make better use of them in the workplace, improving our own performance and that of others. Too many people fail to bring the skills that they have learned in everyday life into their professional life, but that is not really their fault. The environment and culture within their place of work will have a big influence on this, which we will discuss in more depth later. Suffice to say for now, that when a manager fails to deploy these transferable skills, a genuine risk emerges that the full potential of their team will never be realised and an upward performance spiral will not be created. By developing and managing relationships more effectively then, a performance manager can identify and leverage these transferable skills. As with the everyday examples we considered earlier, this approach will identify mutual benefits that become a major contributor to improved performance outputs.

So how should we manage relationships in a business environment? The answer is straightforward. Exactly the same as we do in everyday life, we follow a basic four-stage process, as illustrated below.

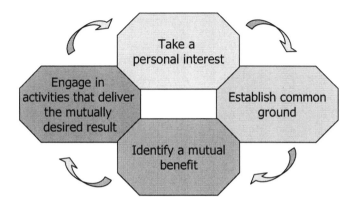

Taking a personal interest starts with getting to know the people in our team and giving them the opportunity to get to know us. This needs to be done in a balanced way or it can have disastrous results. I have seen both extremes. On the one hand there are bosses who stay distant, thinking that being close will make it difficult to manage under-performance or discipline individuals should the need arise. On the other hand there are bosses who get too close to the point where they become so much a part of the team that there is no clear direction, or leadership in existence. Neither extreme will work well towards driving a high-performance culture. Why? The first scenario stifles performance. People feel that their leader is cold and distant, interested only in getting the job done and not in the individuals in their team. This makes it difficult to establish any common ground, or identify a mutual benefit. As a result the team members are unlikely to offer any fresh input or new ideas and they will probably feel that they don't have the freedom to express themselves. This type of manager is often branded in a negative way and eventually their team will seek to do the bare minimum necessary to complete the tasks they have been set. Ultimately key individuals in the team may even want to move to another job where they feel that, working for a new boss, they will be valued more. The second scenario breeds a very different environment, one that on initial inspection appears to be conducive to high performance. However further investigation reveals that despite the impression of a fun, energetic, together team, the lack of leadership and direction means that this is not a productive environment. Whilst the team may enjoy themselves, they also become frustrated by the absence of structure and authority as well as the lack of focus on meaningful activities to progress mutually desired outcomes. As in the first situation individuals are likely to move to a new job with a different manager, where they will be able to grow and develop and have their achievements recognised by a stronger leader who they respect more. To develop effective relationships in our team we must strike a balance between these two extremes.

We touched briefly on the 'relationship bank account' a little earlier, explaining that relationships work by paying in and drawing out. To get off to a good start and to ensure that we begin with a 'credit balance', it is important that, as the manager, we make the first 'deposit'. We cannot expect people to make sense of us – we need to make sense to them. This requires effort and planning. We can start by sharing a little about our background, our previous roles, some of the successes of our previous teams, or individual achievements that demonstrate our credentials as a manager. Clearly we want our subordinates to 'buy' us as a manager, but to begin with they need to 'buy' us as an individual. They need to see that we are authentic and genuine. To achieve this we can reveal some detail about our personal life, for example our likes, our dislikes, our hobbies and maybe our family life – enough for them to start to get to know us and understand what is important to us. They will have formed an opinion about us the instant they set eyes upon us, so the very least we must do is invest some time to ensure that the opinion they form is accurate! If they have an accurate view of us they are far more likely to paint an accurate picture of themselves, which will form a solid basis for a meaningful relationship with them. Taking a personal interest becomes a natural step and will make it easy thereafter to establish common ground and begin working towards a mutually beneficial end result.

It is so important that we take responsibility for this first 'deposit' into the relationship account. Having our intention absolutely crystal clear in our own mind is critical to ensure we create the right impact on those around us. It would be a mistake to believe that we can achieve this by adopting the "here's what you can expect of me – so this is what I expect from you" routine. For a start this approach is cold and impersonal, but more importantly we are not yet in a position where we can realistically expect to make 'deals' with the members of our new team. It is far too early to make our first 'withdrawal' from the relationship account. Only after they have bought into us as a manager and accepted some of our ideas for the team, will they be happy to do a 'deal' around their individual contribution in return. A good leader will keep refreshing this process, just like paying more money into a bank account to replace depleted funds. If we intend to deliver high performance then we are certain to make many sizable 'withdrawals' over time, so we must also make regular large 'deposits' to keep our team motivated.

All of this makes perfect sense if we are a new manager starting out with a new team, but what can we do if we are already the manager of an existing team? If this is the case, we cannot start over with the nice relaxed introductions and well controlled initial impressions as our team already knows us – too well at times, we may think! However, this is not a barrier to moving our current team towards high performance status. It is still possible to develop and manage existing relationships to become more productive using the same basic four-stage process.

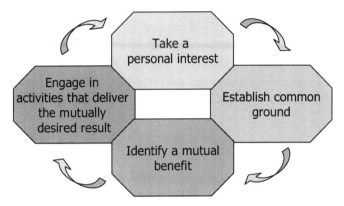

However long we have managed someone, it is never too late to take a personal interest in them. We may find that by doing so a new area of common ground can be discovered. What are their current goals? How do they want to develop their career? What do they want to achieve in the coming year? Or what do they want to achieve more immediately, perhaps during the next two or three months? How do their plans fit in with the plans we have for our team, or other areas of the business we are a part of? This discussion will go a long way to identify a mutual benefit to underpin the activities that will deliver the mutually desired result.

If we have similar dialogue with every individual member of our team we can breathe new life into our relationships with them which will create a stronger desire to improve performance through mutually agreed goals and activities. We increase the 'credit balance' in the relationship account which will then be available for us to draw on as we drive performance forward.

Having looked at how to develop and manage relationships

within our own team, we can now turn our attention to managing relationships with others who do not work directly for us. Very often we find that there are many people who are not directly part of the team we manage who can have a significant impact on our own performance, so it is imperative that we learn how to manage these relationships productively. Peer relationships are a good example. If our goal is to create a high-performing team we will actively encourage the members of our own team to work together to develop healthy peer relationships. We need to do the same. I remember a conversation with a manager who was struggling with this aspect of relationship management. She felt that the relationships within her own team were working really well, but that the relationships she had with her peers in the management team were not as productive. She wanted to do something to improve the situation but was unsure how to go about it. I asked her if the management team had regular discussions about the team vision and goals – unfortunately they didn't. This went some way to explaining why the peer group were not enjoying productive working relationships. They had lost sight of their common ground as a team which meant that identifying mutual benefits for being part of the same team, and working together to achieve a mutually desired result would be very difficult for them to do. We talked about how to re-establish the common ground – the team vision – and then work through the relationship management cycle from there. This would re-invigorate the management team as a whole, enabling them to work together as a team towards their common goals knowing that they would also gain a personal benefit from doing so. Rather than each of them working in isolation with their own individual teams, this approach would make them far more effective as a leadership group.

There are other relationships that we may need to establish or refresh – to bring these to life we should develop a network map.

This involves identifying all the people we want to have a productive working relationship with. We can then challenge ourselves on which relationships are working well and why, where it is necessary to make 'deposits', and where it is appropriate to make some 'withdrawals'. From this we will also identify where we have gaps in our network, and decide how we can fill these by developing new relationships.

By way of example, consider the network map below. This is not an exhaustive template – it simply illustrates the exercise so that we can each produce our own specific network map that is relevant to our circumstances at the current time.

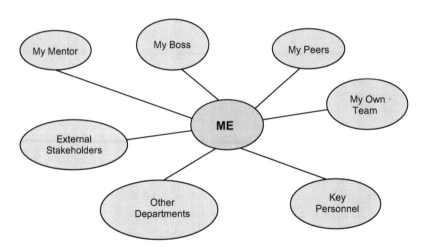

When completing this exercise it makes sense to view ourselves as a company that is aiming to attract financial investors. What is it that attracts investors to buy shares in a company? Generally speaking they want to get a good return on their investment so they will seek out a company that they want to be associated with that meets their investment criteria. For example do they like the company's structure, the way it is managed, its purpose, its activities, its products, and its brand? Investors will also want to be satisfied that the company will make money, and if they see it as a 'safe bet' they are more likely to invest in its future.

If we compare ourselves to a company seeking investors we can ask similar questions to find out whether we, as an individual, are an attractive investment. Is it worth other people 'buying in' to us? Do we meet the criteria of our potential investors? Do they want to be associated with our activities, our productivity and our brand? Will they view us as a 'safe bet'?

The response to these questions will help us to gauge our personal 'stock value'. If we have a large number of productive relationships with a broad range of people this proves that we are the kind of person that others see as a worthwhile 'investment'. They can be confident of getting a satisfactory 'rate of return' so they will happily become a stakeholder in us. This is a good indication that our relationship management skills are developing well, which will benefit our performance. On the other hand if we are finding that the relationships with people on our network map are sluggish and unproductive then it is very unlikely that they consider us to be an attractive investment. We will need to fix this problem urgently. We cannot kid ourselves that the other parties are at fault, or that we don't actually need a relationship with them. In reality, we may need them more than they need us and, if this is the case, we have to make ourselves more attractive to them otherwise they will not invest in the relationship. If we are not creating value for our 'investors' then they will 'sell their stake' in any relationship they have with us, and take their 'investment' elsewhere. This could be the beginning of a catastrophic series of events. If these 'investors' doubt our viability, then there is a very real risk that the members of our own team may no longer believe our 'stock' has a high value either. If they begin to withdraw their 'investment' too, then, just as a company without investors will fail, we simply cannot survive as the manager of that team. If we see any of these symptoms developing we must act quickly and decisively, long before we reach the point where we lose our grip on the team. If that were to happen it would have disastrous consequences to our goal of leading our team to high performance.

Developing and managing healthy relationships is a key part of successful performance management. We need to continually assess the productivity of all the relationships on our network map to ensure that we balance the 'deposits' and 'withdrawals' effectively. Each of these relationships will have a significant influence on the 'temperature' and culture in our team and on our overall performance. We must aim to offer good value to prospective 'investors' all of the time, so it is worth reflecting on our current management style to ascertain how we can develop a more relationship centric approach which will encourage new 'investors' to 'buy' into us. After all the strength of our relationships will have a direct correlation to the strength of our performance.

Understanding and managing reactions

The process of communicating and developing relationships will, by its very nature, always necessitate the involvement at least one other person. As soon as other people become involved, different views and thoughts, principles and beliefs, ideas and goals, are introduced. Therefore we cannot be certain to receive a consistent reaction from everyone all of the time. Striving to develop our communication skill in an effort to get everyone we interact with to act on everything we request of them at the first time of asking is not a realistic blueprint for successful communication. However compelling or convincing we are, it is a fact that not everybody will accept everything we say immediately after hearing it. We can save ourselves from frustration by accepting this fact and aiming for a different goal.

Earlier we mentioned that the communication process involves a transmitter and a receiver. To be *effective* it is absolutely essential that we develop our skills as a transmitter so that we are consistent in delivering clear messages to other people. To become *highly effective* we must also develop a very clear understanding of how the receiver works, and how we can influence the way our messages are heard and acted upon. To achieve this we need some insight into human nature. This understanding will help us to adapt our communication style to each set of circumstances, and tailor our approach to suit individuals. Firstly we need to learn how to anticipate the reactions we are likely to get to our communication, and then secondly we should develop our ability to manage those reactions in such a way that will ultimately achieve our desired outcome.

To begin with we must recognise that whenever we receive a message, an instruction, or some form of feedback, there is a process that all of us go through. None of us are exempt – it is a product of our genetic make up. Of course human nature is not an exact science, so even though there is a generic process involved here, many individual versions of it could become evident when we are dealing with a group of people. It is important that we understand this so that we can prepare for their reactions.

As with many of the topics we will touch on throughout this book, this process has been the subject of a great deal of research. There are some very detailed models that explain the human reaction to any form of change. Elisabeth Kübler-Ross developed an emotional change cycle that explained the way people react to bad news. Her research with terminally ill patients in the late 1960's, identified the emotional states of the people she observed as they came to terms with their ordeal. Interestingly the emotional cycle she discovered is not exclusive to significant negative changes, like facing up to a terminal illness. People follow the same pattern whenever they perceive that they could be negatively affected by the occurrence of change. Even though one of the biggest challenges we face as people managers is the fact that every individual is different, this insight into human nature helps us to see that the general reaction to change in our team will tend to follow a consistent pattern.

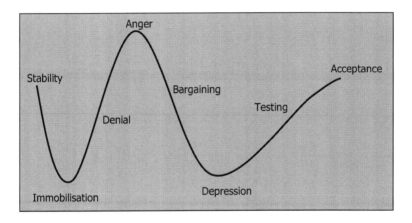

To help make sense of this in performance terms, and support the development of our communications skills as performance managers, we must learn how to recognise the steps within this cycle and how to manage people through these stages effectively. We can adapt the model for use in a business environment by drawing out the four main areas that we should be aware of, noting that the 'bargaining' and 'depression' stages are more likely to manifest themselves as 'rationalisation'.

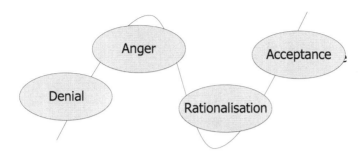

Each of the three stages that precede acceptance involves a range of emotions that are not conducive to high performance. If we want our team to perform at their optimum level all of the time we should ensure that they spend as little time as possible in these three stages. We need them to reach the *acceptance* stage as quickly as possible every time we 'transmit' a new communication, set of instructions, request for a change of actions, or when we provide personal feedback on their own performance.

Some people, by virtue of their own personality, will go through all four stages very quickly – so quickly, in fact, that it may appear that they have moved immediately to acceptance. Certain ideas or decisions we communicate will meet with very little challenge, and again it could appear that the audience has moved straight to acceptance. However, each person will have worked through each of the stages, they are just not as evident when the desired outcome is arrived at so promptly. The challenge for a performance manager arises when the 'receiver', be that an individual or a group, gets stuck on one of the first three stages. If this is not rectified swiftly, and in an appropriate manner, it will have a detrimental impact on the performance of the team.

To illustrate this I recall an example about a small group of people who had developed a belief that it was impossible to deliver the target they had been set in a 35-hour working week. Even though others in the team around them were meeting and exceeding the same target, this group still believed it was impossible for them. They were stuck in the denial stage, and their manager was powerless to help them improve their performance until he could move them through to acceptance. He had tried all the traditional methods of communication he could think of but despite his efforts in coaching them, implementing new ideas to support them, and even threatening them with penal measures, they remained in denial and he couldn't shift their performance. Unfortunately, too many managers get frustrated and give up at this point instead of finding a way to manage the individuals through the process. To achieve the right outcome we have to tackle each stage in turn, which is precisely how we approached this situation. Unsurprisingly, stating that 35 hours was sufficient time for them to meet target, and highlighting that the successful members of the team were proving that fact, made the group angry. That wasn't what they wanted to hear. To fix their performance the issue had to be tackled head on, which included dealing with the anger stage. Once the anger subsided they immediately moved into rationalisation coming up with seemingly endless lists of reasons why it must be somehow easier for these other people, or why their issue had not been fully understood in the first place. It was only after going through this stage too that they could get to the point where they accepted that it was possible for them to meet the target just as it was for everyone else in the team. Having arrived at this realisation they also began to accept that they had the power to positively influence their own performance. Through patient communication their manager was able to guide and support them during their transition through all four stages, and as a result their performance began to improve.

There are at least two key lessons we can learn from this. Firstly, we should plan our communication with the 'receiver' in mind. Secondly we must stay in control of moving people through the stages to 'acceptance' as quickly as possible. This is especially true when we are delivering messages where there may be more resistance to immediate acceptance, or those that are likely to be unpopular. In this case we should test the effectiveness of our communication beforehand by considering all of the options at our disposal to land the message well, and all the possible challenges we will face within the first three stages. This will equip us to navigate safely through the denial, anger and rationalisation emotions, ensuring people arrive firmly in acceptance and are ready to deliver the right performance outputs immediately.

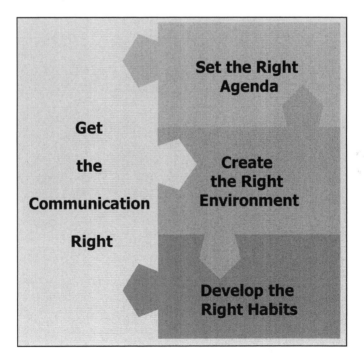

As we move on to explore the other components of our high-performance framework we should remember that our success in setting the right agenda, creating the right environment and developing the right habits will be significantly influenced by the quality of our communication. Our competence as communicators is linked directly to our success as performance managers – communication is the central tool and skill of 'our trade'. Communication is the 'lifeblood' of our high-performance culture.

3

Set the Right Agenda

What's on the agenda?

To achieve the right outcome from any meeting an appropriate agenda needs to be set so that the delegates will understand the reason for convening the meeting, and the reason why they have been invited to attend. Whether we are planning a full day face-to-face meeting or a twenty-minute conference call, we are much more likely to get positive outputs if we set an agenda that provides purpose and structure so that everyone in attendance will point their energies towards the desired outcome of the meeting.

Learning how to use a meeting agenda to better effect is invaluable for us, but even more valuable is the importance of setting the right agenda for our team on a larger scale. If it is our goal to lead our team on a journey towards high performance then careful and serious thought is required about how we set our overall business agenda and how we stay on track to deliver it. Setting an agenda that provides clarity and purpose for our team is vital if we want to build a high-performance culture and achieve long-term success.

It would be easy to presume that setting a business agenda is the domain of executives, senior managers, or those who run their own business. That is not the case though. Setting the right agenda is the start point, the first step of the journey, for all of us who find ourselves in a position of leadership and who have a passion and desire to achieve high performance. It is imperative that we develop the ability to set a clear agenda. How do we do that? What is involved?

We can begin to answer these questions by saying that setting the right agenda in our business is dependent upon clear definition. A television salesperson will tell you that the images on a High Definition TV are brighter and sharper than those on a standard television set. We are told that HD gives very clear, crisp pictures with vivid colours and up to five times more detail which means that the clarity of the picture is significantly better. It is just the same with performance management. It is crucial that we form the habit of communicating in 'High Definition' so that the people we manage are absolutely clear on the agenda we are working to. The more detail and clarity we provide when defining the tasks we expect people to deliver, the greater their understanding will be of what is required of them. They will see the picture more clearly.

What are the areas of our agenda that require 'High Definition'?

Firstly there are a number of strategic aspects. We start by defining a vision for our team along with the values that the members of our team are expected to display. Then we define the plan we will work to, which includes the short, medium, and long-term goals that we will deliver. Our team structure requires definition too, as will the individual roles that are required within that structure.

Secondly there are a number of day-to-day aspects. It is important to define the role responsibilities and objectives for every individual member of the team, clearly articulating precisely *what* they are required to do, *why* they need to do it and *how* they can deliver it. To support them in this we have to be clear at all times on our current priorities and key performance deliverables.

Why is 'High Definition' so important? Simply because it is not realistic to expect anybody to deliver a strong performance if they are not absolutely clear on the requirements of their job and our expectations of them. This is true whether we are asking them to undertake a very simple task like making six copies of a document and handing it to six specified people before 10am, or something much more significant like buying into a five year strategic plan and giving us their commitment to deliver a major part of it. If our aim is to become a highly effective performance manager then we will recognise that whether we are dealing with people on a day-to-day operational level, or at a higher strategic level, it is our responsibility to define the right agenda for our team. Our agenda should be much more than a task list. We have to develop and structure our agenda so that it acts as a frame of reference for people to work within. We demonstrate belief in our agenda by developing a crystal clear vision, a set of values, and collective team goals. These will help everyone in our team to make a positive contribution by delivering the specific and measurable objectives of their clearly defined role. Let's consider each of these component parts one by one.

The vision

Defining a clear vision is imperative. We cannot underestimate the value of a powerful vision. That being the case we must accept the responsibility for developing a vision in our team – although we shouldn't necessarily be the sole contributor to what that vision is. Involving our team can be very valuable if we do it in the right way. This means involving them in defining the actual vision, not just in creating a vision statement – and there is a significant difference between the two. There is a risk that, in an effort to create a captivating vision statement, people can focus too much on the words and less on what the vision actually is, so any real meaning behind those words is lost. In order for people to be properly engaged in a vision they must also be engaged in the meaning behind it. Our vision must be compelling.

Interestingly, a vision isn't something that has to be meticulously planned so that it is realistically achievable. "I have a dream..." said Martin Luther King Jr. – without any mention of strategy or planning. There was no doubt though that the people he addressed grasped the meaning of his vision and were engaged in it.

Our vision can take any form we like as long as we are totally committed to it and we are able to take other people along with us on the journey. Few of us will change the course of history, or run companies that transform the way people work, travel, or shop. Not all of us will reach levels of seniority in the organisation we work for where we become influential in decisions that change the direction of the business. However, every one of us who leads other people must have a vision for ourselves and our team. It is something that will guide, shape and direct our actions in the right way because it is easy to visualise and work towards. This will unify the team, and once we have a team whose members are all pointing their energies, abilities, ideas, and focus in the same direction we become a powerful force.

For example, a few years ago the management team I was working with embraced the vision of becoming universally recognised as a high-performing team. One of the ways we visualised achieving this was to paint a mental picture of a queue of people outside our office building who were all pursuing a position in our team because they wanted to be a part of our success. In reality this was a vision that would never be realised in the form of a literal queue. However it helped us, as a management team, to focus every day on the most appropriate activities that we needed to deliver so that our imaginary queue of people would grow even longer. This made our vision really powerful because we didn't need a 'rule book' that set out a blueprint for our success. We had something much more potent. We had a vision that we could all easily make sense of, which gave us a clarity that influenced our brand of leadership and, in turn, contributed to our high-performance culture.

Of course the real benefit of our vision was for the people who already worked in the team, and it wasn't so much about those who were yet to join the 'queue' outside. Sharing our vision with everyone in the team was very straightforward because they could easily relate to it. They could see that this vision would influence a style of leadership that would ultimately benefit them personally. On that basis they readily accepted their individual responsibility to contribute towards the vision by making our team the sort of team that others would want to join. Creating that responsibility through a simple vision that was easy to communicate meant that everyone could commit to it. As soon as they did our vision was, in effect, transformed into a contract.

The whole team knew that we had a clear agenda for our business and they wanted to be a part of it. People willingly signed up to this 'contract' and recognised that, if everyone played their part to the best of their ability, we would all benefit. That generated buy-in which, from my perspective as a manager, is worth so much more than an over-engineered vision statement that could easily be inaccessible or inexplicable to the majority of the team. We enjoyed similar success when the management team expanded and we evolved our leadership vision into 'creating an upward spiral'. Later we developed this into a vision which could be embraced by everyone in the team, at all levels. The key message is that, if we establish a vision that every member of our team can relate to they will be inspired and motivated to contribute to it in a positive way.

The lesson is clear. We create a vision for our team by deciding what we want to achieve collectively, and how this can be visualised by everyone to harness the power of their combined energy. By doing this we will quickly transform a group of people into a team who are ready to progress on the journey towards high performance.

The values

Once we have clearly defined our vision we can begin to pinpoint the values that must exist in our team to propel us towards that vision. Whilst our vision provides us with an ultimate destination, our values are more like a mode of transport that influences the speed at which we progress toward it. Obviously our values must be closely linked to our vision; however, there is a choice, or decision to be made, over which values will best serve us on our journey. This choice is really important because our values may even determine whether we successfully reach our destination or not.

We can illustrate this by considering our personal values. Each of us has an individual set of values which define who we are, how we think and act, and what we will become in the future. Our values are not genetic; they are established by choice. It is true that our values will be shaped by the things that we have experienced and been exposed to, but however strong those influences are the fact remains that we choose our own values. We could say that our values are effectively a set of promises that we make to ourselves and to other people, and we will be expected to keep those promises. Whether we like it or not we will be judged on how well we deliver on the personal values promises we make.

It is reasonable to conclude that, if we choose the values we want to display as individuals, it must be possible to do the same as a group. A group vision on its own is not enough. Our vision may prove popular with people, but they will also want to know how we intend to work towards it. If they like our vision but do not like the way we plan to get there, then they will not commit themselves to the cause, which means that, even at this early stage, it is very unlikely we will ever reach our ultimate destination. Our choice of group values will influence how many people willingly want to join us on our high-performance journey. On that basis, establishing a team values system that works for the *whole* group is a fundamental part of our agenda-setting process. To be successful we need people to be fully engaged in both the vision and our team values, because we cannot achieve our goals unless we take willing, committed people along with us on the journey.

* How can we create a set of values that will drive us towards our vision?

* How do those values become an integral part of our overall agenda?

* What do we collectively believe in that will bond our team together?

* What promises do we as a team want to make to ourselves and to others that we happy to commit to, however difficult it may become to keep them?

The values we choose as a team may need to be selected in a more deliberate fashion than the personal values we acquire over time as part of our character. Nevertheless these team values still amount to a set of promises that we make to others, and they are promises we must keep. When a team comes together it is important to identify a set of values promptly as we may not have time to wait for experience and exposure to shape them. If we understand the purpose of our values and the role they play in our success we can avoid the risk that we highlighted earlier when we considered the way many vision statements are formed. When defining a set of team values it is very easy to generate a list of words such as excellence, dedication, accountability, adaptability, dignity, unity, efficiency, empowerment, responsibility, respect, fun, bravery, loyalty, pride, passion, honesty, integrity, teamwork, quality, empathy, courage, and interdependence. However this is only a collection of words unless they become promises which harmonise perfectly with our vision. The values we establish must become woven into the fabric of our leadership brand which will shape our character as a group, and exert a powerful influence on the way we perform as a team. When this happens our high-performance journey will gather momentum and we will begin to achieve our goals.

The goals

We cannot claim to have the right agenda in place if we haven't set any goals. Our agenda has to be goal-oriented. Whether they are short term, medium term or long term there must be goals to aim for.

The fundamental difference between our vision and our goals is the way in which they are measured. As we said earlier, a vision might be an aspiration, or even a dream, that may appear almost impossible to turn into reality. Goals are different. They ought to be stretching, maybe even a little scary at times, but they must also be achievable if we want them to have a positive impact on our high-performance culture. Our goals become the foundation upon which we can review our achievements and then set new goals in pursuit of even higher performance.

Our team goals should to be owned by everyone in the team,

not just the leader. This may be a big challenge because setting stretching personal goals isn't something that many people are in the habit of doing. We may find some who set 'new years resolution' style goals – to stop smoking, start saving, lose weight or to get fit, for example – but traditionally these goals don't even survive until the end of January. In fact, research on the topic of goal-setting suggests that as few as 3 per cent of the population actually set and write down genuine personal goals. So it is reasonable to ask, how can we develop a goal-oriented team if, on average, 97 per cent of the individuals we work with don't share a goal driven mindset?

Having already stated that setting the right agenda is all about definition, it is imperative that we take responsibility to clearly define goals for everyone in our team. The performance-related goals we set need to become personal to each individual. This can be achieved by gaining an understanding of the personal motivation of each member of our team, and linking this to their individual contribution to collective team goals. This process will help translate the team goals into the personal goals of those in the team. Once their personal motivation is involved they will be more inclined to set their own performance related goals, which increases their positive contribution to the teams' success. This will provide encouragement for them to set and achieve more personal goals, which will build their confidence and contribute to their growth and development, thereby unlocking strengths and abilities which will contribute significantly towards our high-performance culture. Ultimately we will engender a more goal-oriented mindset within the team.

However, personal motivation is not always easy to identify, and sometimes we may have to find a way to create it, or at least translate it from an emotional state into something that is more tangible. For example, people may say that they are motivated by money when actually it would be more accurate to say that they are motivated by the things they are planning to spend their money on. So to make effective links between personal goals or personal contributions and key business objectives, we have to connect with what the individual actually wants to achieve. This month they may be working for the money to pay for a holiday, next month for a new TV, the following month an item of jewellery and so on. Or alternatively within the next twelve months they would like to have enough money to buy a new car, pay for a wedding, or put a deposit on a house. These goals are tangible and visible, and we can use them to create a physical link to their business performance. To bring this to life some people put pictures on their desks to remind them of the goal they are working towards. I have known managers who create display boards that depict the individual goals of the people in their team. This acts as a visual reminder which helps to maintain high motivation and focus on the day-to-day business activities that will ultimately contribute to their personal goal.

In some instances creating visibility of goals is not quite this straightforward. I remember, a number of years ago, two young men in my team who were both good performers, delivering almost identical results. The only difference between them was that one worked no longer than 8.30am to 5.30pm each day, whereas the other was working from 8am through to 8pm. He came into the office at weekends too, and he was beginning to get downhearted about the amount of hours he was spending at work. It would have been tempting to reach for the time management manual at this point. We tackled it in a different way though by looking at his goals, motivation and personal contribution. He was happy with the contribution he was making, as was I. He was less happy about his personal goals and motivation. We explored why his colleague was able to deliver the same performance in a much shorter time, and we discovered that it was less to do with his time management ability and more to do with his self-discipline. He had a wife and two young children that provided his motivation and shaped his personal goals. To support his family he wanted to earn a certain amount of money now, and develop future career prospects that would enable him to maintain his standard of living, but he also wanted to spend as much quality time as possible with his young family. He set out to achieve this goal, supplying his own motivation and self-discipline. All he needed beyond this was a manager who recognised his personal circumstances and supported him along the way. The result was that he delivered a significant business contribution balanced against his own clear set of personal goals, which meant he was strict with his time. On the other hand, the young man who was working all the extra hours without additional reward didn't have an external motivational driver, or strong personal goal, that generated a similar level of self-discipline. As a result he spent more time at work which created the illusion that he was working harder for the same result. He needed support and guidance to identify some personal goals that would supply the motivation he needed to discipline himself to balance his time in order to achieve them. Having talked it through together we came up with a solution. He didn't have a young family to go home to which governed the time he would leave work each day. He did, however, decide on a clear personal goal to get fit, which we could use to create a similar focus. He decided that, in future, he would go for a run, a swim, or visit the gym, at the end of his working day which gave him a deadline to stick to, and a tangible personal benefit to work towards. This helped him to get all his work done in less time whilst still delivering the same business contribution he had done previously. As a result his motivation increased, his work life balance was restored, his performance remained high – and he got fitter too!

This also illustrates the fact that even very simple goals can be effective in driving the right results. It is important to recognise this point as it is not realistic to expect everyone in our team to have big significant goals, but we do need a goal-striving mentality within our team that will drive us collectively towards high performance. Productive relationships are born out of this environment because everyone has something to gain, not at the cost of others, but in partnership with them. These relationships are certain to drive incremental performance and contribute to our upward spiral.

We said earlier that team goals should be owned by everyone in the team, not just the leader, and we explored how the leader can create a goal-oriented team to support this mutual ownership. To underline the point, let's consider what might happen if the leader's personal goals were to dominate the team agenda. Under these circumstances there is a strong possibility that the team would feel that they were nothing more than a vehicle for their boss to achieve those personal ambitions. How diligently are people likely to work for that boss? It would make more sense the other way around. People are much more likely to work hard for a manager who acts as a vehicle for the success of those in their team. So we should ask ourselves – do the people in our team perceive that we are giving them opportunities to deliver great performance and achieve their own goals, or that we are taking the glory for their hard work in pursuit of our own ambition?

To answer this question we can consider the basis of contract law. The fact that contracts exist proves that people are happy to voluntarily enter a legally binding agreement which obligates them to fulfil their part of the contract in exchange for something that they believe will benefit them. Having established a common ground and a mutual benefit, the parties each bring something to the contract that makes it work. Often this will be something of value to them, but they consider it a worthwhile sacrifice in exchange for what they expect to get in return. By applying similar principles to performance management we can become more successful in driving motivation towards achieving goals. Earlier we likened our team vision to a contract with the whole team. We can strengthen that position further by creating these individual 'contracts'. We may be surprised just how much people are willing to commit if they can see the personal benefit they are likely to gain from a working relationship – it will certainly be a greater commitment than if they feel they are nothing more than an accessory to achieve the goals of their manager.

Identifying, setting, and supporting delivery of the personal goals of others is a key consideration in the 'contract' we have made with them. Our commitment to this investment in them will govern their level of commitment to delivering their side of the 'contract' as they fulfil their role.

The roles

To successfully deliver our business agenda we need to deploy the most suitable people in the most appropriate roles. The vision, values and goals will provide direction, define our aims, and identify the key activities for our team – but however well we have defined all of these aspects there is still an enormous dependency upon every individual in the team to deliver the right results. This is a real test of our ability as a performance manager. Serious thought is required about how we define the individual roles within our team, and who can best fulfil those roles.

To meet this requirement we should periodically examine the structure of our team. Is it flexible and adaptable? If our agenda changes then some roles may have to change too. This could involve either permanent or temporary adjustments. Changing structures or role definitions permanently can be a challenging business, and may require that we make some tough decisions.

When it is clear that changes are required we cannot avoid the situation. Making tough decisions is 'par for the course' where high performance is the ultimate aim.

Sometimes though a temporary re-structure or change of role definition will be all that is required to keep our agenda on track. From time to time we are confronted with issues that we couldn't have planned for. When this happens we should always react in a positive way so that our underlying business goals are not jeopardised. Maybe we only need to change the focus of a few people, but it will still take a brave decision to make that happen, and we must manage them well through the change, regardless of its temporary nature. This has been necessary a number of times in my team. On one occasion we had two months to amend some processes to comply with changing regulatory requirements. It was obvious that a 'business as usual' approach would not achieve the right outcome quickly enough, so we had to take a different route. We re-aligned the roles of about eight members of the team temporarily until we were happy that progress was being made at the right speed. Once we had met the objectives of the project they returned to their own roles. In the cold light of day this course of action sounds obvious, but in a busy workplace, with a deadline looming, the pressure of the situation can sometimes mean the wrong decisions are made – or the right decisions are not made quickly enough. Therefore having a regular review of roles and responsibilities is a good habit to get into. Whether we make temporary changes, permanent changes, or no changes at all as a result of our review, this approach still makes sense. It retains fluidity and flexibility within the team, which means we will be far more efficient and effective. Our high-performance culture is strengthened too as the team develops a 'can do' attitude and are less likely to be fazed by the prospect of change.

The objectives

After we have identified and established the roles we require in our team, and organised them into the right structure, we can begin to set some really clear individual objectives. In much the same way as we have outlined throughout the *setting the right agenda* section, it is imperative that we define individual role objectives with clarity and precision. This is a fundamental aspect of performance management. People will act in accordance with their understanding and interpretation of the instructions they have been given. However clear we think we have been we won't get the right outcome if, for some reason, our requirements have been interpreted inaccurately. If this happens we should really challenge ourselves. How clear was our communication in the first place? How specific were the objectives we set? Did we document the objectives to create a record to refer to? Did we have sufficient rigour around checking understanding? How robust was our follow-up?

Working for a manager who is vague with instructions, but then reserves the right to be disappointed with the results will quickly become tedious. In the main, people have a desire to deliver the task that they have been assigned to a reasonable standard, and they will find it incredibly frustrating if they have worked hard at a task only to be told that they got it wrong. If this happens regularly then it will be impossible to develop productive working relationships in the team. Anyone who finds themselves in this environment will become less motivated and less likely to use their initiative. Performance levels will drop and ultimately people may choose to leave that team in search of a different job. This powerfully demonstrates the fact that individual performance outputs are a direct reflection of the precision with which *we* define role objectives for people, and how effective *we* have been in linking their objectives to our overall business agenda.

There is another pitfall that we must avoid. It is not enough to provide direction only on *what* is required. If people don't know *how* to do what we are asking they still won't be able to deliver the right outcome. It is essential that we provide the right level of support through training and coaching so that our team knows *how* to deliver the expected standard. Our effectiveness in the diagnosis of training and coaching requirements is critical to this process. We cannot afford for tasks to be delayed or hindered in any way. Neither would we want to damage the confidence of anyone in our team, nor expose them to the fear of making unnecessary mistakes, simply because they don't know how to do something properly. We will explore this in more detail later when we consider the impact of 'self-preservation'. Suffice to say for now that having a proactive approach to the training and coaching needs of our team means that we will progress beyond a purely task-focused, transactional style. Embracing the all-important people focus is critical to our goal of delivering bigger and better results through a high-performance culture.

The measurement

We tend to think of measurement in terms of results, or outputs. Results get reported – and rightly so – but the end result is not the only aspect of performance that ought to be measured. By the time something becomes a result it is, by definition, over. So it is not possible to *manage* the results, all we can do is *measure* them. As a performance manager though, it is our responsibility to assign and oversee the actions or activities that will drive the next set of results. By measuring the effectiveness of those actions and activities as well as our rate of progress, we will know whether we are on track to deliver our desired outcome whilst it is still possible for us to influence the end result.

The more specific and precise we have been in the way we

initially set objectives and allocate tasks, the easier it will be to measure ongoing success rather than waiting for the results to tell us whether the actions are working or not.

For example an athlete would not wait to see whether they won a medal at the Olympic Games as a way of validating whether their training methods had worked or not! An athlete measures the success of each aspect of their training plan on an ongoing basis so they know, before the Games commence, that they have put themselves in the best possible position to get the right result. If at any point they feel that something is not working they will immediately adjust their actions in order to influence the result they want to achieve later. Athletes, and other sports people, are really focused on this as they tend to have only a small window of opportunity to achieve their goals. They have relatively short careers, within which many of the major events they compete in feature only once in every four years. They have to be focused because if they miss out at one of these events it is a long time before the next opportunity comes along.

How would our approach as a performance manager differ if we were confined to just two, three or maybe four opportunities in our whole career to get the right results out of our team activities? It is an interesting question to reflect on which leads us to the natural conclusion that we should look more closely at how we approach the measurement of our team activities to ensure they are driving the desired performance outputs. By adapting and changing our activities in response to what our ongoing measurement is telling us, we are able to remain on track towards the end goal.

Our adaptability could include challenging conventional thinking and setting our own higher standards for people to reach. In any business there will be accepted standards, methods, and processes that may have been in place for many years. If we are serious about creating a high-performance culture we should challenge those norms to release greater creativity and give impetus to our upward spiral. Everyone in our team needs to know what our standards are, and strive to compete against the standards rather than competing against each other. I remember speaking with a young man who had become preoccupied with comparing himself to his peers. He felt that others in the team were being offered opportunities whilst he was being overlooked. This had affected him negatively. He had begun to persuade himself that actually he was better than them, and that his manager was not treating him fairly. I pointed out to him that he should be more concerned with measuring himself against the required standards of his own role rather than allowing himself to become distracted by what others around him were, or were not, doing. We discussed a 'performance barometer' that can be used to pinpoint precisely where people are on their individual journey to high performance.

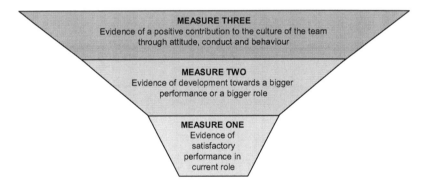

By measuring and comparing relative performance in this way, individual performances support progressive improvements across the team because people begin to focus on their own personal contribution without becoming unduly concerned about the contribution of others. Whilst the first measure will be evidenced in the main by performance metrics, measures two and three prove that we cannot limit ourselves to monitoring numbers. If we measure quality as well as quantity we can strive towards attaining higher standards because the benchmark will be continually raised, and our performance spiral will keep moving upwards. The combined effort of our team in pursuit of higher standards will improve performance outputs and further embed our high-performance culture.

We cannot allow anyone to satisfy themselves that performing below the required level is alright as long as they are doing their job slightly better than the people around them. The defined standards we have set should be the only standards that everyone in our team competes to achieve and is ultimately measured by. To reach these standards some members of our team will have to stretch their performance levels. Others, who may already have attained the required level, will begin to stretch themselves to achieve more, or develop themselves towards a promotion. These positive behaviours will contribute to a culture which drives the collective team performance forward creating an upward spiral, accelerating our high-performance journey.

Self-preservation

At times, even though we have followed all the right steps in clearly defining roles and tasks, as well as offering appropriate training or refresher coaching, we find that, for some reason, the required action is not forthcoming. We can begin to understand why this happens if we explore the rule of self-preservation.

Self-preservation can be summarised simply by saying that if we think something will hurt us we will naturally want to avoid it. It is a common perception that failure will hurt, and because of that, fear of failure is a very powerful driver that can make people do the strangest things. This could even include the deliberate avoidance of clearly assigned tasks or instructions. As mentioned previously – if someone doesn't know *how* to perform a task it will be very difficult for them to deliver a satisfactory result. If this lack of knowledge combines with a fear of failure, avoidance of the task is a very likely outcome and we need to know how to manage this effectively. We may feel that the assigned task is well within the capability of the person we have delegated it to, so to us their avoidance behaviour is illogical and irrational. If we recognise that they are consumed with fear of the consequences of failure we will realise that their mind has begun to play tricks on them. Instead of working through the options available to successfully complete the task they go into damage limitation mode. They are concerned with the challenge they may receive, or the embarrassment that could be caused, by trying to do something but then getting it wrong. At this point the highly charged emotional state they now find themselves in is not conducive to rational, logical decision-making – so they avoid the task.

When delivering presentations I have often illustrated this point by referring to the well-known children's fairy tale, *The Emperor's New Clothes,* in which a rogue tailor cons all the adults, including the emperor himself, into believing that he can make the most exquisite clothing they had ever seen. He asserts that these garments are only visible to the wise, and therefore anyone who cannot see the clothes must be a fool. On the strength of these spurious magical qualities the tailor extorts huge sums of money from the emperor to make him a new suit of clothes when, in fact, he produces nothing at all. He 'dresses' the emperor and tells him and his courtiers how fabulous he looks in his new garments. Of course none of them wants to appear foolish so they completely disregard the logical and rational explanation, the fact that the emperor is naked, and perpetuate the con. They are more concerned about self-preservation, so they pretend that they can see his clothes rather than face embarrassment or ridicule from others. The emperor proceeds to hold a public parade to show off his 'new clothes'. All his subjects react in the same way, pretending that they can see his new suit rather than run the risk of being viewed as foolish by others. The story then introduces us to a young child who clearly has no fear of what others will think of him if he speaks the truth. He points out the fact that the garments are *not* miraculously visible to some and invisible to others, they are simply non-existent. The emperor and the other adults have been deceived by the fraudster who exploited the rule of self-preservation because he knows that, in general, people will not willingly put themselves into a position where they appear foolish or feel embarrassed in front of others.

This is a valuable lesson for us to learn to help make sense of performance management. The reasons for avoidance are never logical, and the excuses for it are seldom genuine, but that is not necessarily the fault of the individual. It is our responsibility as a performance manager to set an agenda that answers the questions *why*, *what* and *how*. Through clear communication people will quickly understand *why* we have set the agenda, and *what* they are required to do to contribute to it. To deliver it though, they also need to know *how*. We must provide the training and coaching they require to be able to do their job efficiently and productively. To avoid the damage that can be caused by avoidance we have to ensure that, at all times, everyone in our team is comfortable with all aspects of our agenda, the tasks that they are required to undertake, and the desired outcome. As long as we keep the communication lines open and regularly check understanding of *why, what* and *how*, the individuals in our team will not be exposed to the fear of failure, and we will not be exposed to the risk of self-preservation.

This checking and validation process needs to be cyclical.

Many people tend to be forgetful. In the workplace we may describe this politely as knowledge fade, or skill fade. Essentially this means that a person can easily forget how to do something if it is not performed regularly. They may have appeared fully competent just a few weeks or months earlier, but if the passage of time means that they lack confidence at the point where they are re-assigned the same task we may find that fear of failure emerges again. This increases the risk that people may even avoid tasks that we think they are familiar with. Therefore, whenever we re-allocate a task we should confirm with the person, or people, involved that they still have the knowledge, skill and confidence to deliver the performance we expect.

This may sound excessively deliberate. However let's reflect for a moment on how people in this situation could be feeling. Most readers of this book will consider themselves to be confident, competent drivers. Maybe we passed our driving test many years ago, and have a long track record of safe motoring behind us. That being the case it is unlikely that we would get unduly nervous or worried when we sit behind the wheel of our car. How different though if we were to return to our car after a long day at work to find a driving examiner waiting for us. The examiner kindly informs us that they will be joining us on our journey home to assess our driving skills against the standards required to pass the current driving test. All of a sudden nervousness and anxiety would kick in and we would begin to worry about all the bad habits that may have crept into our driving over the years. We would fear that we may have forgotten some key elements that could lead to us failing the test. Fear of failure and the pressure we are feeling may prompt us to avoid the situation altogether by refusing to get in our car! How much more reassured we would be if the examiner offered us the opportunity of a brief refresher by way of some 'on the spot' coaching which would verify our knowledge and ability, as well as build our confidence that we will be able to pass the test.

Understanding the rule of self-preservation helps us to develop a deliberate approach to explaining and expressing our requirements with clarity and precision, not only the first time we ask, but every time. We will also recognise the need to develop a clear programme of training and coaching to help people maintain their confidence and competence over the longer term, which will negate dangerous assumptions about their ability to continually meet the required standards over time.

Making sense of this aspect of performance management will also help us to progress our journey towards high performance. Providing clear definition, along with appropriate support, releases creativity and determination. Instead of resorting to avoidance, fuelling a downward performance spiral, our team will be more likely to become proactive. They will go further than the demands of the basic task which will drive performance forward, creating an upward spiral. This 'can do' approach within a team stimulates self-belief which is a powerful catalyst for people to achieve more. We will quickly start to see the benefits. For example, the limiting effect of so-called 'glass ceilings' ceases to be a risk to our performance, because when individuals in the team observe others pushing themselves through the 'glass ceiling' they strive to keep up. As a result overall performance improves because we have created a team culture that encourages progression.

Removing limiting beliefs

One of the best examples of the positive impact achieved from removing limiting beliefs is found in athletics history. It is common knowledge that Roger Bannister was the first man to run a mile in less than four minutes. Before he did so, though, the world record had stood at 4 minutes 1.3 seconds for nearly nine years. There was a prevailing belief that it was impossible to break the four-minute barrier. Bannister dispelled this theory on 6 May 1954 at the Iffley Road track in Oxford, when he recorded a time of 3 minutes 59.4 seconds. This achievement signalled to every other athlete that it was possible to run a mile in less than four minutes. Armed with that knowledge, other runners attacked the four-minute mile with renewed focus. Even though it had taken nearly nine years to break through the 'glass ceiling', once it was broken other athletes immediately developed a 'can do' approach that brought them greater success. As a result Roger Bannister's new world record stood for just forty-six days!

Bannister's sub-four-minute mile was less than a one per cent improvement on the previous best time, but it was the most important 'one per cent' in the history of running a mile. It very nearly didn't happen that way though. Bannister had competed in the 1500m final at the Olympic Games in Helsinki in 1952 and, even though he completed the race in a new British record time, he finished fourth and returned home without an Olympic medal. It was reported at the time that Bannister seriously considered retiring from the sport after the 1952 Olympics knowing it was unlikely that he would compete in the Melbourne Olympics in 1956. Rather than end his athletics career on a disappointing note though, he decided to set a new goal that arguably made him more famous than he would have been as an Olympic medalist. By achieving his goal of breaking the four-minute barrier he had a greater and more far-reaching influence on the performance of others. Roger Bannister removed a firmly established limiting belief. Through his clarity of vision, goal-setting, determination to succeed, and self-belief, he inspired other athletes to push themselves harder than they would have done otherwise. Bannister's achievement earned him a place in history and changed the landscape of athletics forever, which proves the point that it is those people who break through 'glass ceilings' and remove limiting beliefs who create history. If you are in any doubt as to the validity of this statement try to name the runner who was the first to break Bannister's new record – without doing any research, of course!

If we want to successfully create a high-performance culture then we have to work hard to remove limiting beliefs so that we can break through any 'glass ceilings' that may, at present, be a barrier to us reaching a superior performance. Even the minor changes we make, the 'one per cent' differences, will inspire our team to develop a 'can do' approach that will enable them to improve their performance way beyond the levels that they would have set for themselves otherwise. Putting it in athletics terms, they will start to run faster.

I remember being challenged by a colleague who thought that I was setting a target for my team that was impossible to achieve. "Why are you setting them up to fail?" I was asked. Interestingly my team didn't see it that way. We had developed a very different viewpoint. "We won't class missing the target as failure," I said. "We will see getting close to it as success." By aiming high we broke through a 'glass ceiling' and achieved a result that many thought to be impossible. We achieved a better result which we counted as a success, and that is what the team celebrated and remembered. We should encourage our team to develop the mindset that, even if we just miss a stretching target, we will always achieve a great deal more than if we had aimed lower and hit the target. In the final analysis this can never be counted as failure.

Refresh and remind

Setting the right agenda involves clearly establishing our vision, values, goals, objectives, and measurement processes. Next we gain the all-important buy-in from the individuals in our team, and then begin to develop them and stretch them towards greater achievements. To maintain high performance our focus should be on how we keep our agenda on track by becoming proficient at identifying opportunities to refresh the agenda, and remind the people around us of their obligations towards it.

We observed earlier that there are many people who process information in a transactional way, meaning that they see the things they do as a series of individual events rather than as component parts of a higher level strategy. This can become exaggerated in an environment where individuals repeat specific tasks or certain aspects of their role on a very regular basis. Through no fault of their own they can easily lose sight of the overall vision and the goals of the team, instead becoming preoccupied with performing their individual tasks in isolation. There is a risk that this pattern could lead to a downturn in performance levels unless we regularly refresh the agenda, and remind people of the part they play in delivering it. This keeps the real purpose of the team at the forefront of everyone's mind and promotes a cultural mindset over transactional thinking.

- **Why we are here?** Remind ourselves of the vision we are working towards, the values we display, the reasons why, and the benefits this will give us both personally and collectively. Remind ourselves that we all want to be part of it, and that there is a 'queue of people outside' who want to be part of it too.

- **What we need to do?** Refresh our strategy and our goals. Review our current targets and objectives in line with the overall agenda we are working to. Remind ourselves that we all have a role to play, whatever our position in the team is. Remember that every single positive contribution is vital to the success of the team.

- **How do we should do it?** Respond to challenges as if they are opportunities. Use those opportunities to refresh and rejuvenate individual roles, measuring and rewarding successes along the way. Remind people what it is that they personally bring to the team, developing them and encouraging them to stretch their individual contribution to higher levels than they thought they were capable of. Remind ourselves that we can all improve our performance by working together and remaining focused on our vision, our values, and our goals.

The agenda is a brand

We will explore the power of a strong brand in more detail later as we move into the *Creating the Right Environment* section. However it is worth briefly touching on this now as we conclude our thoughts on *Setting the Right Agenda*.

Brand has become increasingly important over recent years, and image has a significant influence over the choices people make. As a result branding is a big business and if consumers don't like a particular brand image they are less likely to buy that product. On the other hand, products that are endorsed by sports stars or other celebrities often become much more popular. Knowing this fact, manufacturers will constantly re-invent and re-brand products to maintain their competitive position in the marketplace. To secure 'buy in' our business agenda should likewise possess a brand image that appeals to people, and part of our performance management role should include maintaining and up-dating our brand. Regularly considering the following questions will help us achieve this.

- Does our agenda promote a brand image that people want to be associated with?

- Have we built a brand that they can trust?

- Is it a brand they will buy into and commit their energy and loyalty to?

- Is it a brand they will invest their time and their skills in?

- Are we flexible when it becomes necessary to re-invent or reposition our agenda to ensure that people are still as committed to it today as they were when it was first launched?

Marketing departments of major companies are acutely aware of the value derived from continually identifying new ways to engender a strong brand that increases loyalty and commitment from their customers. It makes sense for us to do the same within our team by developing a brand that people will remain loyal to, and which underpins our efforts to create an environment that is conducive to high performance.

4

Create the Right Environment

Be environmentally friendly

Our physical environment has always been viewed as important. It is generally accepted that the environment we are exposed to has a significant influence on us. On that basis, the environment we create in the workplace must have a considerable influence on those who are exposed to it. Therefore it is important to find out how we can create an environment that is conducive to high performance.

It would be easy to focus solely on the needs of the business. This is understandable because business needs are very complex and the day-to-day running of a business is very challenging. There are customers to consider, as well as owners, partners or shareholders. There are key relationships to manage with suppliers, contractors, and regulators. Also there are other areas that require serious attention such as legal, social, and economic issues. Understanding and developing the external trading environment demands a huge amount of effort and energy, which could mean that creating an internal environment that is conducive to the high performance of the businesses employees is neglected. Regardless of the tone set at a more senior level, if we are personally responsible for managing people, we must accept that it is *our* responsibility to create the right environment for *our* team. Whether we lead a small team or a large team, doing so will contribute towards driving a superior performance from the people we manage, which in turn supports the overall business goals of the organisation we work in.

This starts with our own leadership style and the behaviours we exhibit personally. I was once told a story about a senior manager whose private office was at the far end of the large open-plan floor where his team worked. Every morning, when he arrived, he would walk through the floor in a relaxed way talking to as many people as possible. He would take an interest in their welfare, what they had done the evening before, or over the weekend. Eventually he would arrive at his office where the door remained open throughout most of the day unless he was engaged in meetings or on the phone. One particular day though, he rushed through the office without speaking to anyone went straight into his room, shut the door, and began his work. At around 11am he emerged to speak with his secretary. Observing the quiet, sterile atmosphere he commented "There's not much of a buzz around the place today, what's wrong with everyone?" The point is obvious. His own actions earlier in the day had created a very different environment to what was customary, and the team had simply reacted accordingly. Consequently their behaviours changed and inevitably this had a negative impact on their performance that day. Fortunately this was just one day in isolation. As a rule the environment in that team was far more conducive to high performance. By way of example though, this well illustrates the point that, as a leader, we set the tone for our team so we must regularly analyse how we influence the atmosphere and the environment that the people in our team experience.

Acknowledging that a bigger performance will be delivered when we create the right environment for people we can understand the importance of developing the ability to be 'on stage'. Being an effective performance manager involves at times being 'in character', fully recognising the 'role' that we are expected to play by the 'audience' – our team. Even though this analogy includes theatrical terminology this doesn't mean that being a performance manager is simply 'putting on an act'. We shouldn't hide behind a management mask. It is important that we reveal our true character and feelings. However there will be many times when it is necessary to control our mood and moderate our responses within the 'role' we are required to perform. This comes through developing awareness that our actions set a tone which will contribute significantly to the environment our team works in, and will have a considerable influence on the performance they deliver.

Performance culture or people culture

Management has been defined as 'getting results through the actions of others', which means that it is impossible for any manager to deliver results without the contribution made by their team. Every manager I have met accepts this logic. However by accepting this we only identify *what* must be achieved as a manager; we do not answer the all important question – *how* will we achieve it?

I walked into an office one day and my attention was immediately drawn to a sign above the manager's desk which read – "If I look after my people, they will look after my business." That was a very clear message, and a strong indication of what the manager of that team believed in. Her willingness to display her intent publicly and permanently was both brave and clever. It was brave in the sense that having made a very open commitment to her team, she gave herself no option other than to deliver on her promise. It was clever in the sense that the people in her team could be confident that she was the type of leader who intended to create an environment that they would want to be part of – so immediately they could buy into her vision. Consequently, everyone started out with a positive frame of mind and they were optimistic about what the future would hold for them as a group. As a result they took their responsibilities to the business more seriously, and over time they became known for delivering great results with a positive attitude and a smile on their faces.

Of course we cannot hope to achieve outstanding results simply by putting a sign above our desk. Our actions must be consistent with our commitments. Promising something to our team and then failing to deliver on that promise would create a very different environment to the one we are aiming for. Any initial optimism experienced by the team will quickly subside and turn into criticism and negative feeling towards the manager. If we want to be a manager who is brave enough to give such a high level of commitment to those in our team, then we must also have the confidence that we can remain true to our people culture all of the time. We should be under no illusion – this will be challenging. Human beings are complex creatures and managing them is a difficult business at times, but the longer-term rewards make it worthwhile. In my view, making sense of how to create a productive people culture is at the heart of making sense of performance management.

There is another side to the coin though. I have come across managers who focus solely on driving performance outputs, working on the premise that people who don't deliver results in this type of environment should be dispensed with as if they are 'casualties of war'. This may appear to work initially, but questions must be raised around the longevity or sustainability of the performance achieved in such an environment. Concerns about how the job gets done would also arise. For example, is there a danger that a culture built purely on forcing performance outputs will lead to cutting corners that may expose the business to unnecessary risks? As well as potential financial or regulatory risks, we cannot get away from the fact that ultimately there will be a negative impact upon people who are constantly exposed to a culture that is focused solely on performance outcomes, and it will only be a matter of time before issues such as staff absence and turnover arise. In extreme circumstances this will create a downward spiral in our business.

I came into contact with a business some time ago that had driven performance outputs aggressively for a number of years. On the face of it sales results were quite impressive; however other elements of the business scorecard had been neglected. Controls were poor which created nervousness and a prevailing fear throughout the team. This was reflected in the people metrics which reported high absence and turnover rates, along with low staff engagement. The people were fragile. Morale was low, and trust was almost non-existent. This proves that if we don't have a people focus at the core of our business culture, we will find it increasingly difficult to sustain high performance through tough trading periods, retain our key staff during challenging times, and grow a balanced business performance over the longer term.

It has to be acknowledged at this point that not everyone in our team will stay with us on our journey to high performance. Some people will not deliver to the required level however strong an environment we create, and it will be better for them to pursue alternative roles that are better suited to their skills and abilities. In the main though, we can be confident that it is possible to influence people to perform better by virtue of the environment we create. So it makes sense for us to build a genuine people culture as the foundation for the environment element of our high-performance framework.

A young manager who wanted to achieve this approached me for some guidance. He had always driven sales-performance metrics very hard in his team which had proved successful in the past, but he was beginning to notice that his techniques were not working as well as they had done previously, and that his team were no longer as motivated. We discussed this in detail and agreed that, to take his performance up to the next level, he needed to adapt his style to suit each individual in his team. It would be necessary to coach them on their own specific needs, rather than maintaining a 'one size fits all' approach to managing the numbers, or outputs, of the team as a whole. We talked about being the type of coach an individual needs us to be rather than adopting the same approach with everyone. Becoming a more facilitative, more discerning, more empathetic manager would be a real challenge for him – but having accepted that creating a genuine people culture would be the only way to achieve greater success, he became determined to succeed. I remember bringing this to life for him by talking about one of his favourite sports, and discussing the type of coach that would be employed by two very different players of that sport. In the example, we used one player who was a very technical player, and another who was a more flamboyant, flair player. We agreed that each player would need a different style of coaching. One would be focused upon detail, routines, methods and techniques – whilst the other would focus more on the psychological approach, positive mental preparation, and discussing tactics for each match. We concluded that each player would perform to their optimum level if their respective coaches supported them in the most appropriate way. I then asked him what he thought would happen to the relative performances of those two players if they swapped coaches for a period of time. He got the point straight away, realising that, in all probability, even though they were world class players their performance would suffer if their environment changed and became less supportive of their individual needs. Translating that into our own everyday setting, we can conclude that the people in our team are reliant upon us choosing to be the type of coach that suits their individual needs. We can also discern that if we make the wrong choice their performance will suffer. By driving purely for performance outcomes, we can easily adopt an approach that may be inappropriate for a proportion of our team. Where that becomes a large proportion of the team we will create a downward spiral, as their performance contributions begin to suffer. On the other hand by managing performance through a people culture we can create an upward spiral by getting the best performance possible from every individual member of our team. This is what he began to do, and a number of weeks later he came to see me again. He was genuinely delighted to be able to report some significant improvements in his team performance. He told me that for several weeks previously his team had failed to reach their weekly sales target, but within two weeks of changing his approach his team had begun to consistently exceed their weekly target. Although previously he had always focused purely on performance outputs, he now had his eyes opened to an entirely different style of management. Creating a people culture that supports a high-performance environment is a very powerful way to drive superior results – and as this example proves, by focusing less on the performance outputs and more on the people inputs, our results can improve dramatically and very quickly. Our next challenge is to sustain this level of performance. To do so, we have to continually enhance our people skills, which will include learning how to manage both formally and informally.

Formal and informal management

Striking the right balance between formal and informal management practice is key. Many organisations provide their management team with a number of tools that are designed to help deliver a people culture. For example, managers are often supplied with one-to-one forms, development plan templates, appraisal documents, annual review sheets, and other paperwork that is relevant to the business they are in. Obviously there are many advantages associated with working in a company that has the resources to develop and supply these tools. However these are only tools which, in themselves, will not influence the culture of an organisation. As we have commented on in an earlier section, the real value will always manifest itself in the way in which we use them. Fans of the BBC comedy series *The Office* will recall a scene in which David Brent conducts a one-to-one appraisal with Keith from accounts, using the standard company template. The disastrous outcome provides much comedy value, but also serves to prove the point that relying solely on a structured, formal management approach is not the most effective way to engage with the people in our team. So the onus is on us to develop our skills to become highly effective at formal management practices such as appraisals and one-to-one meetings. More is involved though; we need to recognise that informal management goes a stage further, and often this is where genuine value is added.

Consider what would happen if individuals could only engage with their manager at a formal one-to-one, or if every time they wanted to raise a question or query they needed to fit it into a box on a form before it could be discussed. As absurd as this may sound, that is how some staff members perceive the formal management processes in their business to be. This became clear to me when I was asked to review some anonymous staff opinion surveys completed by people who worked in a business that I wasn't involved with on a day-to-day basis. From my remote perspective I was able to condense pages upon pages of survey results into one very basic point – there was an absence of informal management. Staff members in that business were happy to confirm that their management team were very diligent in following agreed processes and delivering formal management, but they didn't feel that they were getting any real value beyond that. Rather than feeling engaged in the business they were a part of, the staff were simply going through the motions. In effect they were emulating what they saw their managers doing – following formal procedure, but going no further than that.

It is easy to say that the reason why this happened was that the informal aspects of management were missing – but what is informal management practice, and how can we use it to our advantage? In essence, informal management helps us to cultivate a level of engagement that makes superior performance possible. It is unlikely that a formal management process alone will inspire people to achieve great results. We should look for a balanced approach that helps to create an environment that is conducive to high performance at all times. This calls for flexibility on our part. By testing the 'temperature' in our team we will be able to adjust our approach to tune into the 'high performance point' that is appropriate to the current circumstances facing our team.

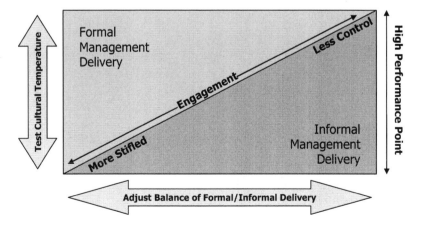

How might we introduce a more informal style to our team environment? We can begin by considering that everyone in our team will probably possess some measure of hidden talent that, as yet, we may not have discovered. Maybe they are naturally strong communicators or motivational coaches in their life outside work. Consider those members of our team who are parents. They have gained a wealth of experience by teaching their children to walk, talk, swim, and ride their bikes amongst many other things. Over time they have developed relationships with schoolteachers and other parents, forming a valuable network of contacts. They may have to organise a complex schedule to balance their work and family responsibilities. All of this takes a lot of skill and a high level of commitment. What about those in our team who are volunteers? Whether they are committee members of local community groups or sports clubs, coaches of sports teams, PTA members or governors at a local school, they have an array of talents and abilities as well as commitment, organisation and personal motivation. Tapping into all of the hidden talent that exists in our workforce and utilising it within our team will enhance engagement and drive higher performance levels. We will never achieve this by following a formal process. It is our informal management skill that will identify and unlock this potential for us. If this sounds like a desirable end result then it makes sense to build effective informal management into our team environment.

An overly formal environment will stifle the natural talents of the people in our team, and they will succumb to being a stereotype of that environment – just like 'Keith from accounts'! Ultimately this means that their effectiveness is limited by the constraints of the stereotype, rather than the wider boundaries of their own ability and desire. If this situation exists in our team then it is essential to break the cycle and get back on track towards a genuine high-performance culture. How can we achieve this? By identifying the real people who are hidden behind any stereotypes that have emerged we can engage people in a programme of development that will enable them to realise their own true potential. This will be a real challenge, and may take time, especially if we have inherited a team who have been managed in an excessively formal manner, resulting in a legacy of negative past experiences. We can be confident that if we successfully meet this challenge the outcome is truly rewarding for everyone concerned.

As the name suggests, informal management is not a rigid structure or set of rules to follow. It is a style that complements our formal management processes to strengthen our team culture. It is an approach that helps us to get the best out of people by creating an environment that affords them the freedom to operate in a more productive way. Doing so will allow them to be themselves in the workplace, exhibiting the full extent of their natural, and sometimes latent, talents.

There are a number of questions that will help us to unlock this potential and uncover the real talents of the people we work with. Balancing our formal and informal management styles effectively enables us to answer these questions and open up a range of benefits that will help our team progress towards high performance.

- Do the people in our team recognise in themselves the natural talents and strengths they possess?

- What natural framework or inbuilt systems do they use to positive effect outside work?

- What models are they using to structure their activities in other walks of life, perhaps without realising it?

- Do they know how to channel these abilities into the business environment?

- What opportunities can we create for people to use their talents in a more effective way?

- How can we link their talent to their role, or other roles where their skills can be utilised?

We can draw the conclusion that a genuine people culture, with a suitable balance of formal and informal management, is the most effective way to develop a high performing team. However, I have heard some managers say that, whilst they agree with this in theory, it will only work in practice if everyone within a team displays the right attitude. It is true that attitude plays a key role in the performance standards people reach, but this viewpoint assumes that it is only worth creating the right environment for people who *already* have the right attitude.

Surely, though, a positive environment is more likely to breed a positive attitude – after all, as acknowledged earlier in this section we are all products of our environment. On that basis we may ask – whose responsibility is it to deliver the right attitude? Should we expect people to be individually accountable, or should we as managers accept some responsibility? There are managers who believe that their job is done once they have imparted the necessary skills and knowledge, and they expect the individuals in their team to supply a positive attitude to enable them to perform at an acceptable level. If things don't go well, very often the first thing to be blamed is the poor attitude of the worker. Inadvertently or otherwise, this implies that any downturn in performance it is the fault of the subordinates and not the manager, but surely this cannot always be the case.

Whilst it is true that each of us chooses our own attitude daily or perhaps even more frequently, we cannot work on the basis that people will consistently choose a positive attitude towards their work. From time to time they won't, but that doesn't mean they are a lost cause. Often we hear managers talking about *skill* versus *will*. Obviously a combination of both is required to drive strong performance, and striking the optimum balance between the two can be achieved through an appropriate balance of formal and informal management. We must guard against an overly formal approach. Most managers tackle *skill* deficiencies through a formal programme of training and development. However when *will* is identified as the issue, there can often be a tendency to question the person's attitude because there isn't an obvious formal solution.

There is no doubt that where a *will* issue develops it can be much more difficult to overcome, but the fact that this presents a challenge to the performance manager is not a good enough reason to lay all the blame on the individual for choosing the wrong attitude. We cannot put this aspect of people management in the 'too hard' box, reach for a trusted performance pro-forma or one-to-one template and satisfy ourselves that, as long as we fulfil the formal aspects of our role, we have discharged our responsibilities as managers. Instead of using the differentiation between *skill* and *will* as a way of pigeon-holing individuals attitudes, we should use it as a diagnostic tool to understand why they have adopted a particular attitude, and then identify the most appropriate course of action to influence the drivers behind their attitude. More often than not this will involve employing an informal management style.

To successfully create the right environment for every individual in our team it is important that we learn how to influence and shape attitudes. It is worth noting here that we are not talking about influencing attitudes that are rooted in the beliefs and values that make people who they are. Performance management is not about restructuring personalities, it is about influencing the attitude people have towards their responsibilities in the workplace and the way in which they can make the best contribution they possibly can to the high-performance journey of our team. This begins by understanding how attitudes are formed.

When information and experience combine, an attitude is created. Simply put, if we are proficient in influencing both the information and the experience that is delivered to people, we will be able to shape their attitude in a positive way. We can express this process as an equation:

Attitude = Information + Experience

To understand this more fully, and to develop our skills in influencing attitudes, it helps if we are aware of how people process this equation. Attitudes are all about thoughts and feelings rather than logic and rationale. Perhaps that is why many managers focus on the *skill* part, but prefer not to deal in the *will* part. It is obvious why more people are comfortable dealing with logic, but once we step into the territory of thoughts and feelings we may believe that we are out of our depth, or that the situation is becoming too personal. This can be a real test of our informal management skill, but one we should never shy away from. We need to find a way to relate to everyone in our team.

Another aspect to be aware of is what happens when one of the attitude drivers is absent. Interestingly, if either the information or experience element is missing then assumptions take their place in the equation.

Attitude = Information + Assumption
Attitude = Assumption + Experience

In both cases an attitude is still formed, but it is now based on something that we cannot possibly quantify or be in control of. The dangers of assumption are well documented, and quite probably at one time or another all of us have had the bitter experience of assuming something only to find that we were very wide of the mark. Knowing the consequences of this, the last thing we would want is for people in our own team to develop attitudes that are formed from assumptions. That would have a devastating impact on the environment in our team, and performance standards would suffer. Managing the way information and experience combine, as well as eliminating the risk of assumption, is a crucial aspect of successful performance management.

I remember being involved in mentoring a young man who worked in a sales team. He had a good reputation and his current manager believed he had a bright future. I was told that his performance was good, but that in recent times his attitude had changed, even to the point of becoming disruptive to the team. His immediate line manager had put a development plan in place for him which included enrolling him onto a formal leadership development programme to support his career aspirations. This had been followed up at one-to-ones, but little or no progress had been made. Added to this he had started to apply for alternative roles in other areas of the company, but without success. This had become a distraction that was affecting him personally, and the team around him. Having already exhausted all the formal options available to him, the manager asked me to get involved to introduce some fresh ideas. I had a very informal chat with the young man on a one-to-one basis. We started to discuss his long-term goals, and where he saw his career heading.

I specifically asked him what he would be doing in five years time, and what he would want to have become known for in the intervening years. He acknowledged that he needed a much clearer long-term goal, however our discussion quickly turned to more immediate planning, and a very personal goal. He had a very young family and was concerned about his ability to provide for them financially. This had led to him setting a short-term goal of securing a better paid job, and he had lost sight of any longer-term goals. He had discarded his personal development plan, dropped out of the leadership programme, and become focused solely upon looking for a new job with a higher salary. The fact that his new goal wasn't working out quickly enough for him had started to have a negative effect on his performance. We discussed this, and agreed that taking focus away from his development plan was probably a catalyst for the negative outcome. In reality, by continuing with the development programme he would actually have put himself in a better place to secure a more lucrative role. In this instance the initial, formal, approach had only served to frustrate both parties. By adopting a less formal approach we got to the root of the problem and were able to get back on track with a better plan. Why was this?

In their earlier interactions the *information* provided by the manager was sound – the development plan was appropriate. However the *experience* element was limited to the very formal delivery of that plan. It didn't reach far enough into the personal drivers and current circumstances of the young man in question, so the equation could not be properly linked together to create the right *attitude*. The lack of an appropriate *experience* meant that the equation could only be completed by introducing an *assumption*. In this case an assumption was made that the development plan would only be of benefit in the long term; whereas this individual felt that he had a more pressing short-term need. It was this assumption that prompted him to discard the original plan and look in an alternative direction. As a result of this assumption his attitude changed, with a negative result. Once we introduced a more informal approach, the *information* on how to progress his career into a better paid role was matched up with an *experience* that was clearly linked to his personal circumstances. The equation was complete and as a result his positive attitude was restored. This example helps to reinforce the point made earlier on about *skill* versus *will*. This young man had the *skill* to do his job. He also had the *will* to succeed which was driven by his family circumstances. However, the environment he had found himself in didn't support this, causing a change in his attitude. It was not a change in his own personal motivation, or will, that prompted him to become more negative than he had been previously. It was the information and experience he was exposed to that had a detrimental impact on his attitude.

Taking this a stage further we can see how all these elements begin to fit together. It is essential that we accept responsibility to influence the whole picture, understanding how this will impact upon our team environment, as well as taking each aspect into account when managing individual performance.

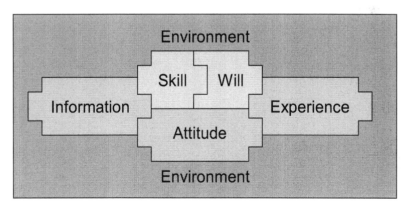

By balancing our formal and informal management delivery we can create individual environments that help people to deliver the best possible performance for them personally. We then sustain their performance by maintaining their engagement – again through a balance of formal and informal aspects.

I remember being approached by two managers who were each faced with the opposite end of the same problem. One had a high performer in his team who had recently deteriorated and he needed to restore the previous performance. The other had a low performer in her team who had recently improved and she didn't want the person to return to past ways. I suggested that they both use the same technique to achieve their desired outcome. This involved mapping out all the contributory parts of the environment these individuals found themselves in now, and of their environment before the performance changes. Everything that had influenced their environment should be included – information, experience, skill, will, and attitude – whether work-related or more personal. Once down on paper it would be easy to see the things that had remained constant and the things that had changed. From this list they could manage the elements appropriately to create and maintain the perfect environment for the team members to achieve their optimum performance. This might involve some formal management intervention, but would be much more likely to be an informal management practice because effectively they would be helping the team members to take control of their own performance with their support.

Both managers returned to me with positive feedback having used the technique to good effect with their respective team members. We can be confident that influencing an individual's environment by balancing the information, experience, skill and will that promotes a genuinely positive attitude is a much more effective and permanent way to drive towards high performance.

We can go a stage further by understanding how individual attitudes will impact on the team environment, and inevitably the other members of the team. I recall talking to a manager who had seen a revival in the performance of his team. I was intrigued to find out how he had achieved this. He told me that a number of people who hadn't been 'pulling their weight' had resigned but those who remained were hard-working people, and he felt he was getting the best out of them. Predictably the subject of attitude came up as he was keen to point out that it was the individuals with a poor attitude who had left. (On the basis they had gone there was little value in debating whether they would have had a better attitude had it been managed correctly, even though this thought did cross my mind!) Instead I asked him about the comparable performance of the people who had remained in his team throughout this period, both before and after the departure of their colleagues. It was clear that the attitude of the remaining members of the team had improved after the departure of the poorer performers. How can we explain this? With the poorer performers in the team both the *information* and *experience* flowing through this whole group was negative. Those who were thinking of leaving weren't performing to the required level, and the rest of the team couldn't see any decisive action towards making changes that they felt were long overdue. Neither did they experience anything that would protect them from exposure to the negative information. This combination of *information* and *experience* had a negative impact on their attitude which produced a dip in their performance too. By this point the whole team was under-performing. Unsurprisingly, once the negative staff departed the negative information stopped, and the team manager began to talk positively about a new start. As he was no longer bogged down in energy sapping under-performance issues, he was now finding it much easier to give those who remained a better experience by investing time with them that had been sadly lacking over the preceding weeks and months. This change to positive *information* coupled with a positive *experience* influenced the change to a positive attitude throughout the team which brought with it an upturn in performance.

Obviously the manager was delighted with the outcome. He really felt that his difficulties were behind him and he was looking forward to a brighter future for his team. "So what's next?" I asked. "I'm going to bring some new blood in to strengthen the team," he replied. "What does your plan look like for that?" I enquired. As I suspected, the plan was not readily forthcoming. By thinking his past troubles were attributable solely to the people who had left his team he had failed to plan specifically to guarantee that the future would be as positive as he wanted it to be. "What is the key driver behind the positive behaviour in your team at the moment?" I asked him. "The time I am able to spend working closely with the people remaining in my team," he confirmed. "What will happen when your new starters join the team?" I continued. He got the point. As soon as the new entrants arrived he would have less time for existing members of the team. Once again, but this time for different reasons, there would be a disparity between the *information* he supplied about the importance of investing time in them, and the *experience* they would receive. This introduced a risk that the attitude of the established staff could dip again, damaging performance as it had done previously. We went on to discuss other risks that could emerge. For example, none of his existing team had worked with new entrants for a number of years, so they had no recent experience to draw on. This introduced a danger that they would rely on assumptions. Would they assume that it was going to be easy to integrate new starters? Would they assume it was going to be difficult? Would they assume that nothing would change?

Would they assume that the training period would last for two weeks, then things would go back to how they were? All of these assumptions could threaten to deteriorate the prevailing attitude within the team, which could begin to rub off on the new entrants – who would probably begin to wonder what type of team they have joined! This could create yet another information and experience mismatch, this time between the information the new recruits had received about joining a great team, and the experience of what they see happening around them. Left unchecked this chain of events would cause a downward spiral. Despite the change of personnel, eventually the performance outcome would be the same as it had been previously.

This reinforces the point still further that the environment *we* create influences attitudes, and it is not solely the individual responsibility of those in our team to choose an appropriate attitude. For example, when a new member of a team who ably demonstrated the appropriate hallmarks of skill and will at their interview begins to display a poor attitude within weeks of starting their new job, we have to question whether it is their new environment that is responsible for their sudden change of attitude, rather than assuming that they are personally accountable for the transformation.

Linking this to our earlier example – we didn't want this to happen to the new recruits of this particular manager, so we discussed his options and came up with an effective plan. It centred on being in control of the flow of *information* and *experience* within the team. That meant leaving nothing to chance. We wanted to apply some informal management practice, so we convened a meeting away from the office in a local coffee house, to discuss the plan with the original staff. The agenda was loose, but the objective was specific. The manager relayed to his team how the months before had been a drain on him and how he was now looking forward to greater success in the future. He confirmed to them how much he had enjoyed spending more time with them, and how pleased he was with the way they had responded. He then talked through the plan for induction of the new starters, reinforcing the fact that it was the collective responsibility of everyone in the team to make them feel welcome and to demonstrate that they had joined the best team they could have wished to join. The team then discussed what the needs of the new recruits would be, and what contribution each existing member of the team could make to the induction and ongoing development of their new colleagues. They realised that effort was required, but by working together effectively over the short term of the induction programme the whole team would be in a strong position to move their collective performance forward over the medium and longer term. Between them they could protect each other from feeling the way they had done just a few months earlier. It became a team effort, a collective responsibility.

Let's just analyse what had happened here. Everyone had the same *information*, delivered in a relaxed yet positive way. Also, everyone owned a part of the *experience*. It was no longer something that was done *to* them – it was something that they were a part of. This meant that mutual accountability for the success of the new entrants was established and the *information* and *experience* elements were consistent, which created a positive attitude in both the established and new members of the team.

By developing a people culture using a mix of formal and informal management we can create a level of engagement that will unlock the true talents of each and every individual in our team and successfully build up positive and productive attitudes that are pivotal to the progress of our journey towards high performance. By adjusting the balance between formal and informal management delivery as the circumstances dictate, we will learn how to find the 'high performance point' for our team and how to maintain an environment where high performance can thrive.

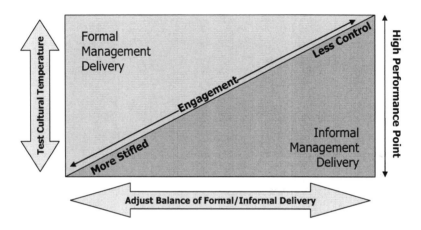

Without a doubt, engaging with the people we lead must be central to our leadership strategy, and there are some key ingredients available that will help us to consistently create the right environment for them.

Our brand

It is generally accepted that people buy people. No matter how strong a product is in its own right it will seldom be capable of selling itself, so the people who sell the product become very important to the retail process. Businesses know that purchasing is a voluntary decision very often based on emotion rather than logic, so they go to great lengths to create a brand image that will appeal to their customers. They support this by recruiting people who are clearly aligned with the brand image, and who they think their customers will like, be happy to deal with, and ultimately buy from.

This people dynamic is true in all walks of life. In the same way as a customer very often 'buys' the person selling the product before they buy the product itself, making connections with other people is the basis for many other productive relationships. We have already established that a high-performance environment is built upon a strong people culture, and this begins when a leader develops a personal brand that other people want to buy into and belong to. All the great leaders throughout history have achieved this, and they are famously quoted as outstanding examples of how to create a powerful leadership brand. Whilst leadership brand is an appropriate starting point, it is our team brand that becomes more important if we want to be the leader of a high-performing team.

Within any team structure there will always be different job grades and salary bands, but it is possible to create an environment where everyone views their role in the team as equally important – and everyone's contribution is viewed as equally significant. It is true that different roles will contribute in different ways, but if everyone delivers their role to the best of their ability and the team works together to stretch everyone's individual contribution, the end result will be consistently high performance. Having an equal status culture is very powerful in bringing a team together so that they gel in a productive and creative way. A 'no stripes' approach works well because it encourages humility within the team. This quality is an important contributor to a team environment where the individuals are more interested in what they can add to the team rather than what they can get out of it. When this begins to happen we see progressively improving performance. Rather than viewing high performance as an individual destination, our team begins to view high performance as a collective journey which is a far more exciting prospect, and they will be eager to explore where it will take them.

On the other hand teams that are made up of very status-conscious individuals are more likely to find that people only want to belong to that team because it serves as a vehicle for their own personal aspirations. In the short term this may appear to work quite well as there will be some strong performance outputs driven through the sum total of all the individual ambition. However this will not work over the longer term because of the differences that exist between a collection of high-performing individuals and a true high-performing team. There are two key differences that are interesting to consider here. The first one is consistency, and the second is the 'multiplier effect'.

Achieving consistency will be a distinct advantage in our pursuit of high-performance goals. There will always be peaks and troughs in any business, which can pose a risk to overall performance. Very often the external marketplace will dictate this. However, where a true high-performing team exists we can protect ourselves to some degree. If everyone in our team is committed to each other and to delivering a collective performance, then we can achieve consistency. Consistent performance outputs are usually a product of consistent management practice, so the end result is totally dependent upon the right kind of leadership – it starts with us as managers. Our brand is the blueprint for the team brand, and by developing a leadership brand that appeals to people who willingly buy into a team ethic based on working together to deliver superior performance we can achieve greater consistency. This is a key benefit of managing culturally rather than through a transactional approach – the result is a high-performance environment.

It is this environment that makes it possible for us to tap into the team multiplier effect. People will work harder towards a goal when they can see other people around them working diligently towards the same end. Those who play team sports know this better than most. If it is obvious that our team-mates are giving their all for the team we are more likely to do the same. Many sporting clichés have developed out of this fact. For example players are expected not to 'let their heads go down' because this will have an adverse affect on the team performance. Instead they encourage one another to 'dig deep' or go for 'one last push' to overcome the opposition. Every time one member of the team puts in that extra effort, others in the team observe this and stretch themselves to the limit too. The effort is multiplied, which enables them to achieve a bigger output from the combined team contribution. This has been described as the whole being greater than the sum of the individual parts.

I once illustrated this in a presentation to a group of managers by asking them to allocate a mark out of ten to each member of their own team. They wrote down the numbers and were then instructed to place an addition symbol ('+') between each figure. They then worked out the sum. "That is the combined performance value of your team" I told them. Then I asked "What do you think about the people you have allocated a low figure to?" Immediately I got the predictable answers about the lower-ranked people – develop them up or move them out. "How much will that increase you team value by?" I enquired. On average by developing the 6-out-of-10 performers up to 8-out-of-10, or by moving the lower-ranked individuals out to replace them with higher-scoring people, each manager added four or five points onto their combined performance value when they repeated the sum with their new scores. That was all it was worth, and for how much effort? "Why don't you keep the original numbers," I suggested, "but instead change the addition sign to a multiplication sign." It took them a lot longer to do the mental arithmetic, but the combined team performance value was enormous by comparison. Yes, it is important that we develop everyone's individual skills up to the highest possible level, but as this illustration demonstrates, we will only achieve genuine high performance when people work together as a team. We gain a clear advantage if we can capture the power of the multiplier effect, which we do by building a high-performing team rather than just assembling a group of high-performing individuals.

I decided to put this to the test in my own team to ascertain how well we were progressing on our high-performance journey, and whether the brand characteristics of a high-performing team that worked well together were apparent. I asked the entire management team how they would define our brand and the style of management we had established, and how this linked to our vision. I was pleased and reassured by the responses they gave. The feedback told me that our vision of becoming a high-performing team was clear in their minds. It was encouraging to find that the team brand was consistent with what we had set out to achieve, and it was evident that they were describing a leadership brand that they were all totally committed to. However we still needed to do more to convert this leadership brand into an environment that enabled consistently high performance across the entire team – that meant engaging with *everyone*. The management team demonstrated a strong desire to do this by providing people with opportunities for growth and development, listening to and valuing the views and opinions of everyone in the team, as well as implementing continuous improvements that would drive the business forward. To reinforce this we developed an engagement framework which included four key components that complemented our high-performance environment. This allowed us to continually test the effectiveness of the people culture we had established, and strengthen it wherever, and whenever necessary by making changes that would keep us on track towards our high-performance goals.

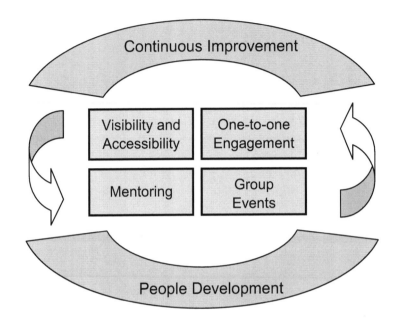

Let's expand on these in turn.

Visibility and accessibility

Leadership is a 'hands on' process. This means being both visible and accessible to the people we lead. Over recent years many businesses have introduced open-plan offices, and as a result the days of managers being shut away in rooms have long gone. However our office layout is not an automatic solution to us being more visible and accessible to our team. We need to be proactive. It is important to look for ways to increase visibility, maybe by joining meetings, sitting in on coaching sessions, or by simply getting off our chair and spending time with the team at every opportunity. It's all well and good to tell people that our 'door is always open', or that they can come to see us any time to discuss their concerns or issues. If we truly want them to do this though, we should make it as easy as possible for them. I have heard people say that they don't like walking around their department because they always return to their desk with a problem that they didn't have before. No doubt that is a slightly 'tongue in cheek' comment. However it is much better to look at these so called 'problems' as vital pieces of information that will help us to run our business and improve the way we lead our team in future. By being proactive we will always find out something that we didn't know before. Then, by acting on this appropriately we will make a positive difference to our team environment. When people see this in action they will use the accessibility we offer them to our mutual advantage. Instead of storing up problems and issues until they start to damage the business, people will raise them in a timely manner, confident that we will take them forward in the right way.

This approach also helps us to reinforce our leadership brand, reassuring people that we are in touch with them and their issues as well the business and its issues. Our interaction makes them feel more involved in the decision-making process of the team that they are a part of. A rapport and trust is developed that, providing we always deliver on the promises we make, will galvanise the team and support our desire to create a culture that delivers high performance.

Mentoring

Whenever taking up a new role I have always sought to get to know the team by holding one-to-ones with every member of the management group – not just those who reported directly to me. Initially this was with the objective of outlining my brand and testing the 'temperature' in the team to understand the existing culture, key messages and activities of the managers. As these sessions took place though. I found that they achieved much more than this, so I decided to make them a permanent feature of our overall engagement framework. Mentoring became an integral part of the development of the management team. I found it very rewarding to be able to support their personal development and growth first-hand, but I also gleaned insightful information about our people, our customers and our business, which meant that, in many ways, I was benefiting as much from these sessions as they were. I encouraged the team to seek additional mentor relationships wherever possible to support their development still further. By subsequently sharing the things they learned from their expanding network we were able to capture the benefit of the multiplier effect as well.

Leaders of other teams that I came into contact with would often ask about our engagement framework. When relating the detail of the mentor sessions I regularly got an enthusiastic response to the idea followed by the question, "How do you find the time to do that?" My answer was always clear: "I haven't got time not to!" I had come to realise that this was a 'self-financing' activity – the management time saved was greater than the time invested. Feedback that I picked up during these sessions was priceless, and often prevented a lot of wasted time dealing with challenges and issues that could have arisen otherwise. As this was a mentor relationship rather than a manager-to-subordinate relationship there was a genuine two-way flow of information. The relationships developed to a point where the whole team regularly asked questions and offered feedback whenever they felt it appropriate, not just at the times scheduled for the sessions. These productive relationships would not have evolved as effectively, or as quickly, if the one-to-ones had been centred on reviewing past performance, or challenging results. Using engagement as the motive we were able to create an upward spiral by proactively developing the team, as well as seeking to solve problems and issues before they arise. More time spent on engaging with, and developing, the whole management team, was a valuable investment that had a significant and positive influence on our team environment. I remain convinced that this is a self-financing activity that, if anything, pays back with interest.

One-to-one engagement

As a leadership team we wanted to expand the mentoring idea. We decided to develop and improve the way all of our managers conducted their one-to-ones. As well as reviewing individual performance and dealing with current issues and development themes, we added a higher-level review of how each person was feeling about their place in the company. We wanted them to have a say in the way our business was run, and by asking them to articulate their ideas we raised the team engagement to unprecedented levels and, at the same time, captured many ideas that we used to progress our business performance. We also wanted them to contribute to the way they were being managed by providing feedback on how inspired and motivated they felt towards delivering the team goals. When we acted on their feedback people felt more engaged, as a result absence and turnover rates ran at all time lows, and the unit was recognised as a great place to work. Our vision was becoming a reality.

This fresh approach to one-to-ones was definitely a key contributor to creating an upward spiral in our team. Even people who historically had been poorer performers began to approach their managers with solutions rather than problems. The management team became more effective too, as they began to manage the individual that performed the role rather than the role that the individual was employed to perform. They learned how to relate to more people, understanding that they all have a valuable point of view. This elicited the background information they required to create better individual environments and influence positive attitudes which subsequently became the catalyst for further performance improvements.

Group events

To expand the way ideas could be generated within the team, and to have an additional positive impact on our team environment, we also introduced a series of group sessions. Some were regular fortnightly events. Others were held quarterly, half-yearly or annually. The key point though was that they were designed to include everyone in the team so that absolutely everybody could become part of the team brand. We wanted to nurture the sense of belonging to something really worthwhile.

The idea behind the fortnightly 'coffee mornings' was very simple, but was still incredibly powerful. Basically we brought a small group of people together, six to eight usually, from different areas of the team. Sometimes those who came didn't know each other very well even though they worked in the same building, so getting them together was, in itself, the first big benefit. There was always a cross-section of newer and more established members of the team, as well as some managers. These sessions supported the visibility and accessibility plan, as I got to know the team much better by spending time with them in small groups. I heard views direct from the 'front line' in an honest and straightforward way which would seldom materialise in big groups where the audience tend to be reluctant to talk candidly, or may be less comfortable to speak up at all. I was able to test the effectiveness of the communication flow within the business, and hear first-hand experiences rather than waiting for them to filter through the management team. At the same time those attending felt they had a say in our business and a viewpoint that was valuable. They knew that they were being taken seriously because the time had been scheduled exclusively for the purpose of listening to them.

I know a lot of managers who have held similar sessions in new teams as a way of introducing themselves and getting to know their team. However, much like the mentoring concept, the real strength of these sessions came through making them a regular feature, and equally, this investment had a fantastic rate of return also. To capture the full benefit, all the points raised in these sessions must be addressed and regular updates communicated back to those who were present. It is imperative that we deliver tangible and visible action from the feedback and ideas we receive. This builds credibility and trust in our team brand, and maintains a healthy two-way communication flow. A word of warning though – it is easy for these type of sessions to become 'talking shops', or they might even develop into an ego boost for the leader. If this happens then the true value will be lost, and the events could even become counter-productive.

The less frequent events were more focused around continuous improvement. Managers at every level ought to be aware of their own development needs and learn how to take advantage of any development opportunities that present themselves. However they may need help, and first-time managers especially need support in this area. Newer managers have the greatest need for development, but are probably least equipped to know how to secure it. The transition into management is very difficult, probably the most difficult career transition of all. Moving out of a self-managed role into a role where we are responsible for the performance of a whole team presents a real challenge. For some reason though, despite their importance and their relative inexperience, in many businesses this group of managers remains an underinvested section of the workforce.

We wanted to fix this, so we designed a programme of development days to build competence and confidence in the key areas of leadership and performance management. We deployed interactive workshop-style events, as well as coaching days and assessment centres. We opened up the world of psychology with the support of some well chosen external consultants. The activities and formats were varied, but all of these events were based on at least one of the facets of our high-performance framework – get the communication right, set the right agenda, create the right environment, and develop the right habits.

We very quickly realised that there was another underinvested group that demanded our attention. Every team manager had a deputy, and whenever the team manager was absent this deputy 'took the reins'. On reflection this happened more often than it had appeared upon first inspection. With holidays, courses and other commitments a manager could be away from their team for as much as ten weeks of the year. Put another way this meant that the deputy was responsible for managing a team twenty per cent of the time. In response to this realisation our Deputy Development Programme followed 'hot on the heels' of the Leadership Development Programme. Not only did this support our business performance, which depended heavily upon the deputies in the absence of their manager, it was also a great way of creating succession and grooming our future leaders.

We didn't forget the rest of the team. We set up team away days to support their development, and social events for them to relax together and get to know each other on a more personal level. Wherever possible we included family members in the social events so that they could buy into our team brand too. We knew that it wasn't possible for people to respond to the demands of working in a high-performing team without the support of their family. To provide a higher level of support at home, family members needed to know what we were all about as a team and see our brand in action. I have always believed in this approach, but it was proved beyond doubt by a comment I heard after one of our family days, when the wife of a manager who had only recently joined our team said that, for the first time in over twenty years, she felt as though her contribution to his performance had been recognised.

As with all these things there is a risk attached. People very quickly get used to the standard of living their environment affords them. Once we begin to enjoy a higher standard of living it is very difficult to go back to how things used to be. If anything it becomes more likely that we will want to enhance our standard of living still further. How many of us would willingly sell our car and buy a cheaper model, or sell our house and buy a smaller one if we didn't have to? It is much more likely that we would want to buy a better car, or a bigger house. Recognising this aspect of human behaviour we can accept that the same will be true with the 'standard of living' afforded by our team environment. People might acknowledge that the environment we have created for them is better than other environments they have worked in previously. However they will still want their 'standard of living' to improve year on year. This is a challenge that takes constant effort on our part, but we will not necessarily have to bear all the responsibility for this ourselves. If our team brand is strong then the team will naturally want to contribute to 'standard of living' enhancements themselves, because they want the brand they are associated with to go from strength to strength. This introduces another key component of a high-performance culture – pride. Pride that makes people feel a sense of belonging is an essential ingredient in creating a strong team brand. Once people begin to feel proud of the team they belong to they will take pride in their work, pride in their results, and pride in the success of the team as a whole. This makes pride another key driver of the multiplier effect, and a significant contributor to our upward performance spiral.

The emergence of pride

Once genuine pride is evident our team brand begins to evolve into something that is really tangible. Unique team language, banter, nicknames, and 'in jokes', all begin to develop. These are very powerful in our bonding and branding process. There are a few dangers that we need to be aware of, but as long as we are alert to these, and act accordingly, these elements are an essential aspect of building a strong team. One area where we need to be alert to danger is how we induct new members into our team where the 'common language' already in use may be unfamiliar to them. We cannot afford to alienate anybody who is new to the team; after all, we want them to 'buy' the brand and become proud of it too – not become instantly confused by it. We should always be careful when it comes to nicknames, recognising that what some may see as a term of endearment, others could view as offensive. Similarly it is important to take steps to ensure that team banter remains tasteful and doesn't overstep the mark. I recall the experience of a young lady who had gained a reputation for having a 'sexy' voice. To begin with this was jovial, good-natured banter, which she took in her stride. Over time though it began to 'wear a bit thin' and she became quite upset. Fortunately, the team environment was such that she could air her concerns honestly and the team stopped teasing her. Had this gone unchecked though, the result could have been disastrous and the team brand would have been undermined.

When harnessed in the correct way, team language, 'in jokes' and appropriate banter will strengthen our team brand and have a more significant impact than we may think. I realised this when I received an email from a colleague who I had worked with about ten years earlier. It was written in the same style of communication that we had used in the team we had both been a part of, and even included a couple of the phrases and jokes that had evolved as part of our team brand all those years ago.

Remarkably his email would have lacked any real meaning to anyone who hadn't been part of that team, but to me it made total sense and brought the brand back to life. It reminded me of the names and the faces in that team, and everything we had achieved as a group. Most significantly, it convinced me of the power that is created when we develop a strong team brand that instils pride in its members. In this case that brand was so powerful that we were still able to relate to it ten years later!

Giving attention to the physical environment we create is very important. First and foremost our physical environment needs to be clean and tidy. A dirty, scruffy environment where broken equipment and badly maintained décor is tolerated is hardly the domain of a high-performing team that will take pride in its work. Once we have got these basics right, we can continue to develop many aspects of our physical environment to contribute positively to our team culture. For example, most of the equipment we use on a day-to-day basis can be branded to become individual to our team. Regular office items like mouse mats, lanyards, diaries, calendars, pads, and pens, can all be personalised. Whether that's done through a distinctive colour scheme – my team all wear bright pink lanyards – a picture, or a logo like our upward spiral graphic, or even a mascot, like the soft toy giraffes we have around the office to encourage everyone to 'stick their neck out' if they have an idea, or an issue, to raise. These items serve to identify the team, the people who are members of it, what they stand for, and the pride they have in the brand. Once we have established our tangible branding we can use it on everything we produce for our team, such as on internal communications, meeting agendas, wall displays, course material, training binders and so on. Team branding that is visible throughout our physical environment will reinforce the team identity and enhance the sense of belonging and pride.

As people see these things come together their sense of pride develops to the point where they begin to work harder to maintain the brand image of the team that they belong to. They view being a part of it as a privilege. The last thing they want to see is its demise, so they defend the team where necessary, and they tell other people how great it is. This serves to enhance the brand further and really establish a strong and healthy team environment where our performance spiral will maintain its upward momentum. This can have a surprisingly powerful impact on people who are not even part of the team, but who may have been observing from a distance – possibly whilst they are lined up in the symbolic queue outside! I remember receiving an email from a manager who had only recently joined our team promising me that he would "live up to the pink lanyard". He must have known that he was buying into a brand that was worthy of the effort that would be demanded from him, and he was already proud to be a part of it.

Who is in our team?

Once people buy into our team brand they will look for opportunities to enhance it further. We are talking about our team environment here, so this goes beyond using technical skills to perform tasks in the most efficient manner. This is about utilising individual personality traits and emotional strengths to contribute to the high-performance culture in our team. We can achieve this by understanding how each person in our team can play a part, and then encouraging them to use their individual strengths to make a positive difference.

Lots of research and analysis has been done over the years on the subject of personality types and team dynamics. It is very likely that, at some point, we will have been through a process of psychometric testing to help us to understand our own personality, or to help our team-mates learn how to put up with us! The theory behind these models can be very complicated because there is such a diverse range of personality groups, and many more variations within each one. Whilst it is not necessary to be an expert, it helps if we have an understanding of the personalities in our team, including our own, and how these can work together effectively to achieve the best results. We should also prepare for any potential 'clashes', arming each member of our team with the right level of self-awareness and sufficient understanding of the other characteristics that are present in the team around them.

This was a lesson I learned at a time when I was managing a relatively small team that was spread over a large geographical area. The individuals in the team worked in different parts of the country and had never worked together previously. Their roles involved high level stakeholder management and demanding relationship management, which suggested that we really needed to be a strong team that interacted well and supported each other in a positive way. However obvious this may sound, it was not easy to achieve. We faced two key challenges. Firstly, it took a lot of effort to get the team together in the same place at the same time, so we didn't spend much time together as a group. Secondly, we were working so hard to build close relationships with other people and their teams that we weren't investing in our own team environment. As a result we were not working effectively as a team ourselves. We were missing an opportunity to consult with each other, and rely on each other for support – albeit at long distance.

It became clear that whilst we all shared a vision, goals and objectives, we were working as individuals. Our team values were not strong enough to create a productive team environment which would focus more on shared responsibility and collective performance. Once we realised this we decided to invest some quality time together as a group to analyse the personality types in our team and make sense of how we could bond these together effectively to develop a stronger, more dependable team environment. We used this time to assess the challenges we faced as an itinerant team who hadn't had the luxury of getting to know each other by working together closely on a day-to-day basis. This included gaining a clear understanding of how we could begin to benefit more fully from the broad range of skills, abilities and experiences we each brought to the team. The time we spent together exploring this had an extremely positive impact as we began to develop an awareness of each others thought processes. This helped improve our productivity because we were able to influence each other more constructively by 'getting onto the right wavelength' much more quickly. Consequently team discussions generated better quality ideas and a broader range of solutions. This was a big step forward. In the past these discussions had been shut down too quickly, or even dismissed out of hand, simply because the topic presented, or the way in which it was presented, didn't immediately resonate with the thought process of everyone in the team. The real lesson here however, is that these principles don't apply only to peripatetic teams. To successfully create the right environment in any team we lead, we should take steps to ensure everyone gets to know each other well, has a high level of understanding of the different personality types, and is able to develop strong working relationships throughout the team.

It stands to reason that similar behaviour groups will naturally get on better together, whilst contrasting types may find communicating and working together more of a personal challenge. However it would be wrong to think that this logic presents us with an easy route to build a successful team. We have already discovered that a group of high-performing individuals cannot necessarily combine to create a high-performing team. Likewise, assembling a team of people who all naturally display similar personality traits is not the answer. Whilst such a team may get along famously, it is unlikely that they would generate enough diversity as a group to identify a full range of solutions or ideas that will deliver optimum performance. I once heard it put like this – "If two people in a team always agree on everything then one of them is dispensable." We can conclude from this that diversity is a prerequisite if we are striving for high performance, but it will present a challenge. The more diverse our team is, the more diverse the personalities will be – and the more difficult it may be to learn how to manage them, both individually and collectively, to ensure that they work in harmony to perform at the right level.

Gaining a greater awareness of the individual characteristics present in our team may alert us to the fact that certain gaps exist. If we feel this could be detrimental to the make-up of our team we must address the matter in order to maintain the right balance. This includes being honest about our own personal characteristics, to the extent that we are willing to acknowledge any gaps in our leadership style that we may want to look to others in our team to fill.

Understanding personality types may also help us to better understand an individual's source of motivation and their personal drivers. It is impossible to be a successful performance manager if we don't have the ability to motivate other people, so it is important to find out exactly what these individual drivers are for everyone in our team. This isn't a complex process. Once trust and honesty exist it is very simple – we just have to ask them. We shouldn't be surprised if they are not motivated by the same things we are, and we shouldn't try to convince them that they ought to be. Rather, we demonstrate to them that because we understand their personality and their drivers we accept their point of view, recognise where they are coming from, and then allow this to influence the way we manage them. Doing so will help us to develop productive working relationships that support the continuous improvement of every individual in our team.

Continuous improvement

A team of motivated people will naturally want to improve. By developing a continuous improvement culture we will add impetus to our upward spiral.

We will only achieve this if we are proactive. We cannot rely on passive experience as a means for personal improvement. Gaining experience is important, but it is not the same as continuous improvement. It is possible for people to feel that they are gaining experience over time without achieving any demonstrable personal development or exponential growth. I once heard a story that highlighted this point forcibly. It was about an individual who found himself in the unfortunate position of being made redundant from an organisation where he had worked for more than ten years. He entered the job market to secure an alternative role in the same industry, convinced that his ten years experience would stand him in good stead with prospective employers, and give him an advantage over other applicants with less experience.

At one interview he attended he was asked the predictable question about what he could bring to the organisation he was seeking to join. He confidently responded that it was his ten years experience working for a blue-chip company in the same industry. At this point the interviewer asserted that what the candidate thought of as ten years experience was, in fact, his initial period of two years experience multiplied by five. It may take a moment to fully appreciate the significance of the interviewer's challenge. In essence he was stating that what the candidate believed would have given him a competitive advantage over other applicants was not a benefit. In fact, in the interviewer's eyes it was a disadvantage.

This teaches us a valuable lesson. We need to be able to demonstrate development and growth as a result of our experiences. We cannot merely rely on the passage of time which, in itself, may not provide any real evidence of continuous improvement. Of course it is true that we will always learn new things as time passes, but that will happen as a by-product of getting out of bed every morning. Passive learning will not be sufficient for us to operate at the pace necessary to maintain high performance levels. Continuous improvement involves much more than simply repeating the same experiences over and over again. It is about developing and stretching ourselves, and providing opportunities for those in our team to do likewise. With our high-performance goal in view, it is crucial that we establish an environment where continuous improvement can thrive.

In his book *The Empty Raincoat*, Charles Handy uses a series of overlapping sigmoid curves to illustrate the life cycle that can be applied to organisations, products and indeed individuals. To achieve constant growth, a new sigmoid curve needs to be introduced before the trajectory of the preceding curve begins to decline. We can apply this strategy to continuous personal development.

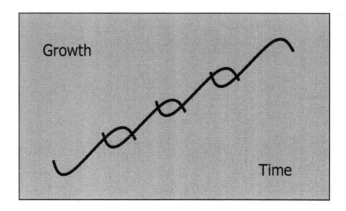

If we want to capture the benefit of continuous improvement within our team we must learn how to manage these cycles effectively. Our skill as performance managers is tested here as we will need to demonstrate forward thinking, initiative, and impeccable timing. We cannot afford to delay the introduction of a new improvement curve for too long or we will find we have lost the motivation or desire of the individual to continue on their development journey. They may have become bored, or find themselves 'stuck in a rut'. Neither can we risk introducing the next curve too early, as the individual may feel pressured to absorb new ideas before they have grasped the preceding development theme. We can set out a strategy for continuous improvement by introducing new challenges at the most appropriate time, as represented by a series of sigmoid curves. To implement the strategy though, we require a greater understanding of the process for embedding the personal development within each of the individual sigmoid curve cycles which is represented by a 'stepped' progress towards competence.

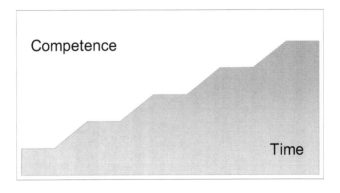

This highlights the difference between a continuous improvement strategy on the one hand, and practical planning and implementation on the other. Making sense of this will help us to build effective individual development plans, and supervise people appropriately throughout the process so that they progress successfully towards their development goal. To that end, the development process needs to have clearly defined 'steps' that divide the continuous improvement journey into manageable stages. Our role as a performance manager is crucial to the effectiveness of this process. To optimise the progress people make we will need to gauge how long they should remain on each 'step', giving them sufficient time to consolidate their learning before offering the right amount of encouragement to advance to the next 'step'.

As an absolute minimum people want to feel competent to succeed in their role, but if we want to build a high-performing team we will have to stretch them beyond competence. That means mapping out an individual high-performance journey for everyone in our team. If the environment we create for people provides them with sufficient development opportunities, and the motivation to succeed, then the collective performance of the team will increase.

Identifying development opportunities for those in our team is a key aspect of performance management. There are a number of avenues available to aid us. Personal development plan discussions are perhaps the most obvious. These must be scheduled regularly and should focus on specific individual goals and personal motivation to pinpoint a continuous improvement journey. A structured training framework is another avenue. We can source training events that are designed to develop generic day-to-day skills, or more specific targeted training to address individual knowledge or skills gaps. We can also develop people by exposing them to a higher level of training than their current role demands. Doing so will assist their continuous improvement beyond competence in their current role and may help them to prepare for a future role which carries greater responsibility. Another opportunity is mentoring. Having a mentor relationship provides a different perspective on how to improve performance. This can very often accelerate personal development through exposure to learning from a more diverse range of experiences, ideas, skills and techniques that have been used to good effect by others. Coaching is another obvious method, and we will look at how to get the best out of this tool in a later section. There are a broad range of opportunities. Identifying and making use of every possible avenue will engender a continuous improvement culture in our team. To capture the benefit of this culture we must maintain the motivation of everyone in our team so that they have a constant desire to continually improve.

To help with this we can introduce 'stretch', which is a central feature of continuous improvement. Stretching ourselves in different ways, including testing ourselves outside our natural 'comfort zone', will contribute to our growth and development. Understandably, some people have an inclination to avoid this, after all our 'self-preservation' instinct generally steers us away from uncomfortable situations. So we may ask – how can we create a team environment where 'stretch' is expected, and accepted, by everyone as a vehicle for their continuous improvement?

I learned the answer to this question from my eldest daughter when she was five years old. I returned home after meeting with her schoolteacher to find her eager to hear what he had said about her. I was very proud to be able to share that her teacher had given a glowing report which, naturally, she was delighted about. I was really surprised though, when the first question she asked me after hearing this was, "How can I improve?" which could appear, on the face of it, to be quite a negative response to a positive report. However, we can draw a different conclusion if we analyse this from the perspective of a five-year-old. She enjoyed the feeling she got when she knew how proud she had made her parents, the confidence she gained from knowing her teacher thought highly of her, and the sense of satisfaction she felt from achieving a great result. She wanted to feel like that again, and she seemed to know intuitively that she would have to improve, or stretch herself, to do so. Her desire to learn and improve was instinctive. As is the case with most children, she had an inbuilt need for continuous improvement.

Unfortunately as we grow into adults it is all too easy for us to lose that instinct. As we have discussed previously, we can fall victim of the fear of failure and our 'self-preservation' instinct can take over. Knowing that this is a natural human tendency our responsibility as performance managers is to introduce 'stretch' in such a way that people will find it rewarding, not frightening. Our aim is to create an environment in which positive behaviours and personal growth are rewarded with praise and encouragement so that the people around us feel good about their achievements. This feeling motivates them to stretch themselves towards further development, in precisely the same way that came naturally to them when they were children. If people feel good about the progress they are making then they will want to feel it again. Their confidence increases and so does their contribution. In future they will be less fearful of the fact that stretching themselves can feel a little uncomfortable. If the environment we create is safe and rewarding, then they will look for opportunities to grow and develop, which in turn will mean that our team consistently delivers a superior performance.

There is a potential challenge that we should be aware of, and be prepared for. We will find that there are people who are happy to remain in the same or similar roles, for a number of years. They could perceive that continuous improvement is only important for those whose goal is career progression, so they are likely to place less emphasis on their own personal development. However, to contribute fully to our high-performance environment we need *everyone* in the team to be committed to continuous improvement. Also, we want to protect such people from the risk of gaining passive experience without evidence of any real development – as highlighted in the example cited earlier. When agreeing development objectives for these individuals we could make a link to their level of job satisfaction, the value they add to the team around them, their contribution to the bottom line, or their reputation with customers. In some cases we could even make a link to something in their personal life outside work.

I faced this situation when a manager who had a great pedigree and a very strong reputation joined my team. Understandably I was delighted that he had decided to join my team because I knew he would add value. He showed great initiative, had a good depth of knowledge, and he possessed a broad stakeholder network. Developing him further would be a challenge, and I was ready for that. However I hadn't envisaged that his personal motivation would be a bigger issue. To my surprise I found out at our first one-to-one that, despite all the impressive hallmarks he displayed, he was actually very de-motivated. We spent a long time exploring the reasons why this could be the case. At the root of it was the topic of continuous improvement. He had developed a mental block towards personal development. For example, he didn't see the benefit of having a personal development plan because, at that time, he had no career aspirations beyond the level he had already reached. Some previous managers he had worked for had focused on continuous improvement as a means of developing towards more senior roles, but taking this approach had left him disillusioned about the whole personal development and continuous improvement process. Taking this into account, setting the right plan for him was difficult. His skills were already highly developed for his current role and as already stated, he had no immediate desire to advance his career. However, we both needed to see his motivation return. We achieved this by looking closely at his personal drivers to construct a plan that was individual and relevant to him. The plan still focused on continuous improvement, but for reasons that had meaning for him personally. This created a new focus that helped him to enjoy his current role more fully and, at the same time, contribute in a really positive way to the team around him. He bought into the concept of continuous improvement and recognised its importance as a component part of developing a high-performance culture.

This example reinforces the fact that building appropriate individual development plans is crucial to making sense of performance management. To be successful, people need to be engaged in the process of their own continuous improvement. A plan that is forced, contrived, or simply there for the sake of having a plan in place, is unlikely to succeed. The development plans we set must be focused on the individual and have a personal significance for them so that they are motivated and fully committed to their continuous improvement journey. There are no hard and fast rules to follow here, and there is no need for any over-elaborate templates that could complicate matters. We just need to build a *plan* that is *personal* and *developmental*. We should always commit the plan to writing, and then monitor progress at regular review meetings to decide together what the next steps on the journey are.

Motivation, incentives and rewards

A high-performance culture must be, by definition, motivational.

As leaders we may be personally motivated by the pursuit of our team vision. In an ideal world this same driver would work for everyone in the team. Unfortunately this is unlikely to be the case all of the time. Sometimes people may feel that there is a conflict between striving to deliver the business vision and simply getting out of the role what they want for themselves – which could be something as basic as their next bonus! If we don't harmonise these business and personal factors there could be a negative impact on the level of motivation in our team, as people begin to pull in an individual direction rather than working to achieve collective team goals. Our skill is required here to help people see that by working together, everyone in the team will benefit personally. They have the opportunity to achieve their individual goals, whilst they continue to deliver their combined business objectives as a team.

I remember having a conversation with a young manager who was feeling slightly guilty about the fact that she wanted her team to perform better so that she could earn more money. She was in the process of saving up for a deposit on a house and was very excited about buying and moving into her first home. This goal was a sound basis for personal motivation which provided her with a very strong driver to increase performance. However, she was struggling to see how she could use this to motivate her team because it was a very personal goal, not a shared common goal. Her skill as a performance manager was being significantly tested. There was a risk that, if her approach was wrong, she could easily 'switch people off' and cause a performance downturn in her team. She wanted to talk it through to see how we could translate a situation that had potentially negative consequences, into positive performance management that would deliver the desired outcome. The first thing we discussed was whether personal financial gain is an appropriate driver for a manager. The answer has to be yes. Everyone possesses their own personal motivations; as managers we are no different to the individuals in our team in this regard, so there is no need to feel guilty. Her personal driver was simply a vehicle by which she became more motivated towards delivering the team vision because she knew that would reward her financially. The next step was to translate *her* reason for being motivated into a reason why *the team* could be motivated to work towards a higher performance that would earn her a bigger bonus. To achieve this, each member of her team needed to have a similar driver based on their own individual goals. We agreed that by identifying their personal goals and inspiring them to achieve these, the people in her team would have a greater incentive to deliver a bigger performance. Ultimately everyone would benefit. We can conclude that there is no harm in forming our own personal motivation based on selfish drivers, but we cannot use *our* personal drivers directly as a way of managing performance in our team. Instead we should find *their* individual drivers and use these to inspire high performance.

This becomes much easier if we develop a leadership style that moves the personal motivation of others. Our delivery needs to be engaging so that those in our team do what *we* need them to do, but because *they* want to do it. To achieve this we have to develop our awareness of the different individuals within our team and use this knowledge to influence the way we interact with them. For example, if we are managing a really driven individual we may need to do little more than channel them in the right way. We would want to avoid the risk of stifling them through overly formal management, which would reduce their effectiveness. Instead we should harness their drive but focus it in the right direction by using a more informal style. It may be that we only supervise at a distance, but if that means they achieve their optimum performance then we will ultimately benefit. On the other hand there will be individuals who don't have a high level of natural personal motivation. They are certain to have a 'button' that can be pressed though, and once we find it we can work with them towards establishing a new goal that provides them with sufficient motivation to achieve more than they were doing previously. This may prove to be a little more difficult and we may be required to adopt a more formal approach to begin with so that their new found motivation doesn't waver.

This highlights the importance of managing people in different ways. To be effective we should plan and prepare in advance of any discussions, working through different scenarios and outcomes to arrive at the right solution for each individual. Understanding the 'what's in it for me' factor from their standpoint will help us to work out how we can get on their wavelength, and find a perspective that has real meaning for them. As the earlier example demonstrated, we also need to be adept at translating potentially negative situations into positive thought processes that will motivate others to deliver high-performance outcomes.

Identifying, creating and nurturing personal motivation for everyone in our team will drive our upward spiral. Once people become self-motivated they will begin to supply their own positive energy, rather than looking to us to renew their energy on a regular basis. This creates even more upward momentum to drive our progress towards becoming a high-performing team, and protects us from the real threat of a downward spiral which occurs in teams where people need constant management attention to maintain their motivation. We cannot allow this to happen because it will seriously sap our energy. As a permanent reminder of this point, I bought a battery for each member of my management team and asked them to keep it on their desk and look it regularly throughout the day. This may seem a strange request on the face of it, but the analogy of comparing a performance manager to a battery works well. When batteries are fully charged they contain energy, but with use they run out and go flat. Their stored energy can only be used once, and then they must be re-charged or replaced. As managers we are very similar – once we have used our energy we need to re-charge. We cannot afford to squander our finite supply of energy on negative tasks or negative people. It is far better to be 'energy efficient', wherever possible pressing one 'button' that turns six, eight, or ten 'lights' on. If high performance is our goal we need to get the most out of every drop of energy we expend, so we should always channel it in a positive way, fully focused on driving positive behaviours that contribute to the motivation of everyone in our team. The result will be that their combined energy will be channelled towards driving performance, rather than being wasted on unproductive activities.

From time to time we may need something extra to boost motivation. Perhaps during difficult trading periods, or when the team is faced with a specific focus, it may make sense to introduce a special incentive. Whenever we use ad hoc incentives it is important that they really hit the mark, so it helps if we are creative. Achieving this can be a challenge, especially in a large or diverse team. We cannot always rely on the 'old favourites' that may have worked well in the past. In general terms, a tried and trusted formula cannot be ignored. However when we use incentives to drive motivation, more often than not, we need fresh ideas. I was once told about a team that had become immersed in the belief that people will 'run through brick walls' if there is a bottle of wine or a box of chocolates on the other side. This approach had worked well for them in the past, and no doubt there are times when this idea may still work, but as with any idea, if it is rolled out time after time it becomes stale and will no longer drive performance as effectively as it once did. I did some research with the team and I found their feedback very interesting. The same sort of incentives had run for so long that it had got to the point where they felt as though they were being 'bought', not motivated. Hearing this was quite astounding because it did appear to be an unreasonable reaction – after all, they were still materially benefiting from what was on offer. Even so, that was how they felt about it, so maintaining that approach simply would not work. This clearly proved that even financially-based incentives can backfire if the team environment is not conducive to superior performance. This team, just like any other, could not be 'bought', and they were desperate to see something fresh that would inspire them to improve their performance. Whether or not their thought process was rational wasn't the real issue – however their reaction clearly signalled that a new approach was long overdue.

As well as being creative, our incentives must be inclusive, so that they are effective in motivating everyone in our team. We want to create an environment that encourages *everyone* to strive towards high performance so that we deliver incremental benefit to the bottom line. Recognising this, it is essential that our incentives create an opportunity for everyone to benefit and thereby encourage every member of the team to stretch towards a bigger performance.

One way to be genuinely inclusive is to look for ways to reward effort and behaviour, rather than focusing solely on performance outputs. Where appropriate this may include recognising the effort people have put in, even if the end result they have delivered is not exactly what we wanted. When it is possible to do this we create greater motivation towards learning, development and personal growth. Ultimately this will have a positive impact on their longer-term success.

Most of the things we learn whilst we are growing up are as a result of making mistakes and then trying again until we get it right. If we hadn't received the right amount of encouragement and reward for the effort or the behaviour we demonstrated on the way to success, we may not have persisted long enough to achieve a positive outcome. Anyone who has children will recognise the importance of this. When a child is learning to walk or talk they make many mistakes, but the child's parents encourage and reward every improvement, often recording the progress the child makes towards the ultimate goal. Once a child starts to get the hang of walking unaided or speaking with a limited vocabulary, it still has a long way to go before it can walk and talk like an adult. However, the encouragement the child gets along the way provides motivation to make the extra effort needed to achieve further progress. People enjoy watching children develop because the effort they put in doesn't come in a forced or resentful way – it comes with enthusiasm and belief. Every small achievement becomes a platform for bigger improvements, until ultimately the child's 'performance' goal is achieved. As adults we still go through the same learning process. By offering encouragement through rewarding the effort that is made, and the positive behaviours exhibited along the way, we will create the motivation required for those in our team to continue to progress until they are capable of delivering a bigger performance goal. There will be more people who believe that they can achieve more, which will contribute significantly to our upward performance spiral. Interestingly, a good example is how this works in the military reward system which tends to be based on effort and behaviour. A soldier who displays courage, bravery and valour during a military operation is rewarded for those behaviours. How else would the armed forces retain the level of motivation required for that soldier to return once again to the heat of battle and put their life on the line for others?

To become equally as effective in the way we reward people, it is essential that we understand the person we are managing, and then manage the whole person – not just the side of them we see at work. This may sound strange at first but it is a key aspect of successful performance management. I remember once working for a manager who couldn't understand why I wasn't motivated by the same things he was, and why I didn't feel rewarded by the incentives he had on offer at the time. For some unknown reason he translated that into a belief that I wasn't motivated, which was, most definitely, not the case. He needed to understand that not only is personal motivation very different for all of us, but it does not necessarily remain constant over time. It can change as our personal drivers differ at various points in our lives. At that particular time my own family circumstances had changed significantly. This didn't make me less motivated, if anything quite the opposite. I was no less effective in my role, neither was I any less committed to the team. I just needed to be managed differently at that stage. This example demonstrates precisely what is meant by managing the whole person. Earlier we identified that understanding personality types gives us an insight into how best to motivate people – now we can take this a step further. By taking an appropriate level of personal interest in people, without prying intrusively into their private lives, we will be clear on the best way to motivate and reward them at any given point in time. It is imperative that we do this in a way that works for them – after all, we haven't really rewarded someone if they don't *feel* rewarded!

It is appropriate to conclude the section on *Creating the Right Environment* on this note. It well sums up that the only way to deliver sustained success is by building a happy, motivated, and engaged group of individually managed people into a genuine high-performing team who are capable of delivering consistently superior results. The next question we must address is – how will we sustain this? The answer lies in the habits that we develop.

5

Develop the Right Habits

Creatures of habit

Human beings are creatures of habit. If we travel to work on public transport we will see the evidence every morning. For example, when I arrive at the railway station for my daily commute I notice the same cars parked in exactly the same spaces as they were the day before. When I reach the platform I notice that the passengers have all taken up their usual places, ready to board the train using the same door they use each and every day to sit in their usual carriage. Then they pass the time on the journey the same way as they always do, whether that is with a book, a newspaper, an MP3 player or by catching up on their sleep. These rituals are repeated day after day, and they are in all probability only the beginning of a series of rituals that continue throughout every other activity they are involved in for the rest of the day.

All of this proves that, by our very nature, we are comfortable with habit. It also proves that once we form a habit we repeat it automatically and with unerring accuracy, because habits are unconscious behaviours. How aware are we of our habits? Are they good habits or bad habits? How can we identify whether they help or hinder our individual performance effectiveness?

In our role as performance managers we are required to go a step further. What are the habits of the people in our team? How productive are they? How can we help them to develop really good habits?

Practise, practise, practise

The key to forming a habit is repetition. In many aspects of life repetition is passive, so some habits are formed without us even knowing. It is different when we want to deliberately create a habit. To achieve this we need to be conscious of the initial action, or reaction, and then generate sufficient repetition ourselves. We do this through practice. The more permanent we want the habit to become, the more practice we have to put in. To illustrate this we can reflect back on some of the habits we form when we are very young. For example, how many times did our parents practise crossing the road with us before they let us do so unsupervised? They kept on practising until they knew that we had formed a reliable habit, a routine that we would never forget, knowing that our very life could depend on it. They did the same with many other life skills that we have carried forward into adulthood.

Most of the good habits we form in childhood are a product of parental coaching. Parents may not readily view themselves as coaches to their children. However they most definitely are. Think of the number of times a parent has to repeat a point to a child before it finally becomes a habit. This repetition is a key aspect of coaching and it plays an important role in developing the right habits. It is probably fair to say that, as a general rule, all of our good habits are the product of a form of coaching. Therefore with a strong enough desire, and some effective coaching, we can form new good habits, and even reverse our old bad habits.

Sports coaches will be the first to agree with this. They recognise the importance of developing really good habits that will stand the test of time and also stand up under pressure. I heard one coach use the term "Train hard, play easy", another – "Don't practise until you get it right, practise until you never get it wrong." We may also have heard the phrase that emerged out of England's Rugby World Cup victory in 2003 – "Thinking Correctly Under Pressure" or T-CUP. Whilst all of these are slightly different, the point they are making remains the same. If we form winning habits in a safe environment they will not let us down when we are faced with a pressure situation. Practice is the key to this because the more we practise something, the more it becomes part of our subconscious behaviour, to the point where we can rely on that habit becoming our natural instinctive reaction. Sports coaches instil winning habits in the athletes they work with because they know that so many other factors can take over when the pressure is on. Those factors are often outside an individual's control. For example in many sports the opposition, the spectators, and the weather, are all factors that could influence a performance outcome. However these cannot be directly controlled by those involved in the game. The coaching process is designed to help the players control the things that *are* controllable. This prevents their performance becoming contaminated by the distractions around them, thereby enabling them to perform to the best of their ability – which is what we expect to see from a professional athlete. I have often talked to the teams I have worked with about the difference between professionals and amateurs. People are always quick to spot the financial gulf, but ignoring this obvious difference, the basic distinction between the two is that professionals practise more than they play, whereas amateurs play more than they practise. Having a professional attitude towards practice and coaching in our business environment will pay dividends. Similar to sporting events, there will be many occasions when pressure arises from factors that are outside our direct control, and when this happens, just as is the case for a professional athlete, we too want to perform to our full potential. We want the confidence that our actions, reactions, and judgements, are totally reliable. This will only happen if we have programmed our intuitive response through practice and repetition.

We will be more successful if we can convert productive activities into habits and support the people around us to do the same. If we find that we are continually required to remind our team to deliver even minor tasks, then we will have run out of energy long before we reach high performance. By helping them translate basic core actions into routine habits, these key activities become automatic and we will be able to divert our energy towards bigger challenges that will contribute towards a higher performance.

Developing the right habits will serve us well, and doing so is critical if we are to reach our high-performance goal. So we might ask – what are the habits we should develop to make further progress along our high-performance journey?

Make being lucky a habit

This may seem a strange one to start with because it would be easy to think that it is impossible to make luck a habit. We may think that a person is either lucky or unlucky. This belief is dangerous though, because it can lead people into a mindset where they fail to take control of their own outcomes. If we simply believe that people who enjoy success are lucky then we will never take decisive action to achieve personal success. We will either wait for our own 'lucky break' to come along, or we will unwittingly consign ourselves to underachievement in the belief that we are not as fortunate as other people.

We may ask – is luck simply chance or good fortune, or is it possible to 'make our own luck'? It was once put to me that luck is what happens when preparation meets opportunity, and by that definition we can conclude that it is possible to 'make our own luck'. Successful people invariably make the most of the opportunities that they are presented with. They are able to do so because they are well prepared and ready to identify any opportunity that they can capitalise on. To the casual observer it may appear that they were lucky because they happened to be in the right place at the right time. However a more careful analysis may reveal that, because they were well prepared, they deliberately put themselves in the right place at that precise moment. If we want to make being lucky a habit we should strive to be well prepared so that we spot every opportunity that arises, and have enough confidence to seize those opportunities and turn them into success.

Let's put this into an everyday business context. If the salesperson who makes the most sales calls also achieves the best sales results it wouldn't be fair to attribute their superior performance to good fortune. In reality they gave themselves every opportunity to be successful by performing the right activities. It stands to reason that, by making more calls using a well prepared sales pitch, they are likely to convert more of their calls into sales. So 'luck' does happen when preparation meets with opportunity.

There are ample opportunities around us all the time which we will benefit from if we are well prepared to take advantage of them. Unless we are looking for a specialist niche, it is unlikely that we will have to influence the 'opportunity' half of the equation. The other half, 'preparation', is the element that we really need to learn how to control and influence. I have often asked my team to "put themselves in danger of doing business". It always raises a smile, but in a few short words it sums up the importance of being prepared for opportunities around us that will bring success. The best way to prepare ourselves for every opportunity is to build up a catalogue of well rehearsed routines, or models, that we know will work. We won't have time to plan a new reaction to every opportunity that arises, so we are reliant on the good habits we have practised in the past, knowing that they will not let us down when we call on them.

Models that work

Over recent years troubleshooter-style television programmes have become more popular. Whether it's turning around a failing restaurant, reviving an ailing retail shop, or helping parents to control unruly children, we enjoy being entertained by the celebrity experts who go into these challenging situations and turn failure into success.

As well as entertainment value though, there are valuable lessons to be learned from the process that sits behind their achievements. It is true to say that the experts involved in these programmes are brilliant. They are talented, successful people who possess a track record that proves their credibility. We are not expected to match their ability, but by observing the process they follow we can tap into their expertise. One of the secrets of their success is that they understand the importance of using models that work. They stick to a proven formula, relying on processes that they have developed, knowing that they can use these repeatedly to deliver great results.

If we want to emulate their success it makes sense for us to develop a range of models that are proven to work. This will increase our confidence, knowing that we can rely on these habits to deliver our high-performance goals. By developing winning habits in the team around us, we will similarly build their confidence and ability to deliver great results. As we have already established, effective coaching is the key to forming such habits in others, so our coaching model needs to become one of the strongest, if not *the* strongest, of our habitual routines. There are many coaching models that we could turn to, but which one should we follow to ensure that our coaching brings out the best in the people around us?

The best way to learn how to be a great coach is to observe a great coach in action. If we analyse the routines of the 'troubleshooters' referred to earlier, we quickly see that they all follow a similar process that can be summarised in the following six steps.

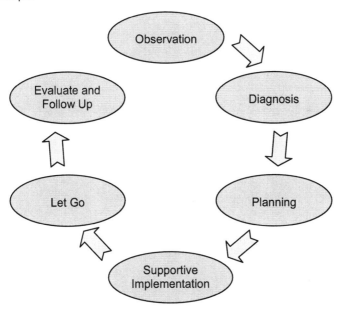

Let's explore each of these steps in more detail to work out how we can make this process a habit.

Observation

In this stage it is vital that we gather accurate information and record evidence of what we observe. Detailed evidence is critical as our findings will need to stand up under cross-examination by the person, or people, we have observed. It may be difficult for them to accept our feedback at first. They may become defensive and try to disprove our findings. Therefore the more evidence we have, the easier it will be for us to paint an accurate picture of the traits and behaviours we have observed. This will help people to accept our feedback and respond positively to their coaching need.

It is essential that we balance the use of our senses during the observation process, watching and listening in silence and without interference. We must not get involved at this stage however difficult it may be to resist. The findings from our observation have an enormous influence on the quality of the coaching experience we will subsequently deliver, so we need a true and accurate view of the current skills and abilities on display. If we get involved too early, we will not be able to gather enough evidence to make an accurate diagnosis, and then the ultimate benefit of the coaching process will be lost.

There are a number of ways we can undertake observation. The most obvious is direct observation of specific people performing specific tasks with a view to coaching them as individuals. However we can also develop a more general observation style that is more focused on the identification of new coaching opportunities across our team. With this in mind it makes sense to spend as much time as possible observing our team at work. This isn't necessarily a time-consuming activity. Even though there are times when we are desk-bound, we can continue to observe the things going on around us. To make the most of this opportunity it is a good idea to use different desks in different areas of the work place. Whenever I have done this I have found it beneficial to see routine day-to-day activities as they happened, rather than just the snapshot view on offer when undertaking regular tours of the office. Building up a picture over time helps us to deliver a more effective coaching experience which is targeted accurately at the development areas we have observed.

It is worth remembering that our observation is not restricted to finding evidence that supports the need for remedial actions. We can also gather evidence to identify and develop the good habits that people already possess. Even though I wasn't aware of it until much later, I learned this lesson from one of my early sales managers. At the time my individual sales performance was good, and seeing my name at the top of our performance league tables told me that I must have been doing something right, so I continued with what I felt was a winning formula. However, if I had known specifically which aspects of my role I was delivering most effectively, I might have been able to achieve more. Not only would this have improved my individual performance; the overall performance of the team I was a part of would have increased too. Although this was a missed opportunity to help me improve back then, inadvertently it taught me a valuable lesson that I have benefited from since – namely, that it is important to observe people doing what they are good at, and to tell them why it makes them successful! This is another aspect of managing the whole person which supports a cultural, rather than transactional, management style. Encouraging people to make the most of their individual strengths by observing existing good behaviours and then coaching them into really strong habits will drive an even better performance from those who may already be performing to a high standard. When this happens our performance spiral moves upwards at an even faster rate.

Diagnosis

In the diagnosis stage we present the evidence from our observation to the person, or people, we are coaching, and share with them the conclusions we have drawn. This shouldn't become a guessing game – we should simply present our findings so that we can begin to diagnose the areas that are to be addressed through the remaining stages of the coaching process. It is important that the diagnosis is undertaken in consultation with whoever we are coaching to obtain their agreement to the required actions, and to secure their buy in to the planning stage which follows. This can be challenging when people are reluctant to accept that any changes are required. Whether we want to coach for remedial, or for developmental purposes, we are not automatically guaranteed a positive reaction to our diagnosis. Many people have a tendency to think that they are 'just fine as they are', or that they are unable to change, having behaved in a certain way for such a long time, so they may take some convincing that coaching is necessary at all. Whenever individuals, or teams, become entrenched in a 'comfort zone' like this, they will be unable to deliver outstanding results. To support our high-performance culture we need to reach a point where everyone in our team reacts positively to honest feedback, knows how to handle constructive criticism, and are willing to change their behaviours if necessary. Any work we have done to instil a continuous improvement culture will support this aspect of the coaching process because it will help to create a climate where diagnosis of coaching needs is welcomed positively and, at times, actively invited by those in our team.

Plan

Once we have reached agreement that action is required, we should then draw up a development plan. As we have covered earlier, there are no hard and fast rules or prescribed templates for the plan itself – to be effective we simply need to adhere to some common-sense guidelines and apply a blend of formal and informal management. To begin with, each of the parties responsible for delivering the actions designed to address the diagnosed issues should be engaged in the planning process. We should always include some commitment from ourselves. By doing so, we create mutual accountability for the actions and a shared responsibility for the desired outcome, which makes for a much stronger plan that has a greater likelihood of success. I remember speaking with an athlete once who told me that on the days he didn't feel motivated to get out of bed early to go training he would remind himself that his coach would have had to make the same effort, getting up just as early to be there to support him, and he didn't want to let his coach down. This mutual accountability spurred him on through the difficult periods, even more than visualising his long-term goal of winning a medal at the Olympic Games. We should never underestimate the power of being an integral part of the planning process, and having a shared commitment to the coaching cycle. Our personal involvement can be just as important motivationally to the people we coach as any longer-term goals they may be aiming for.

Once we have agreed the development objectives we will work towards together, they should be written down. As well as increasing buy-in and commitment to the desired outcome, this provides us with a document that we can refer back to as many times as necessary during ongoing review and progress updates. The mutual responsibility we create at this point strengthens this part of the process because people will realise that our coaching forms part of a supportive relationship which will help them to achieve their personal development goal.

Supportive implementation

The supportive implementation stage relies heavily on strong two-way communication. As the coach we must be very clear on how the plan we have designed should be implemented, and the person being coached needs to be honest with us about how comfortable they are with the new skills and techniques they are developing as they progress through the implementation stage.

One way that this can be achieved is through demonstration. In my view this is a key element of coaching that is often overlooked. A number of managers have proposed to me that, in their opinion, demonstration is nothing more than a camouflage for *telling* people how to do something, in other words insisting that they do it our way or not at all. Keen to understand the alternatives I always ask what they would recommend instead. Often a process of supportive questioning is suggested, which is intended to help individuals reach their own solutions and achieve more buy-in. However, it is more appropriate to do our questioning in the earlier diagnosis and planning stages where we are exploring the most suitable course of action, and securing buy-in to the proposed plan. When it comes to the implementation stage, people naturally prefer to be given a clear explanation of how best to deliver the plan, which could include being shown how to do so. This is where demonstration can be used to good effect, without any negative impact.

On the other hand, when demonstration is overlooked in favour of the facilitative questioning approach it can backfire spectacularly. An endless stream of questions where no firm conclusion is reached only serves to frustrate both parties. The coach keeps searching for a different line of reasoning, but the person on the receiving end is very often left thinking – "What do you actually want me to say? If I knew the answer I'd already be doing it!" Unless we are a highly skilled counsellor, or a psychologist engaged in high-level behavioural coaching, the questioning option may not always get us the result we are looking for. For that reason, the right answer is to show, or demonstrate. Indeed the television 'troubleshooter' coaches we referred to earlier are great exponents of demonstration. We also used the example of parents who, more often than not, will show their children how to do something new before allowing them to attempt it for the first time. It is the same in sport. Coaches will demonstrate how certain skills or techniques should be executed – for example, it is far easier to show someone how to swing a golf club correctly than to ask them a series of questions in the hope that they will work it out for themselves!

We can conclude that if we demonstrate effectively, the 'penny will drop' more quickly to help people realise how the skill we have demonstrated will benefit them. If delivered in a supportive manner they won't think we are telling them to do it our way. Rather they will feel more confident to 'have a go', and will ultimately employ the new skills and techniques they have been shown to great effect by adapting them to their own style.

We must remember that an important aspect of supportive implementation includes creating a safe environment for people to practise in. Whilst often ignored because of their unpopularity with many people, role-plays are often the best way to practise in a safe way. For example, why would we risk getting something wrong in front of a customer, or client, when we can practise over and over again with a colleague until we know we will get it right when it really matters? The supportive implementation stage needs to involve as much practice as is necessary to embed new skills and techniques as well as build sufficient confidence to be able to deliver the required performance level after the coach has walked away. Remember – "practise until you never get it wrong"!

Let go

Once the person being coached has enough confidence to 'fly solo', it is important that we walk away and 'let go'. This supports the view that *showing* is very different from *telling*, because having satisfactorily demonstrated the new skills we allow people time to adapt these to their individual style, and embed them as a habit that really works for them. This is another example of how we can stay in control of positive outcomes without being a controlling manager who wants to have a hand in every action or activity along the way.

'Letting go' is a really important part of the coaching process because it allows people the opportunity to test new ideas and experiment with techniques that they will ultimately adopt as their own routines. We must allow them to work through this process without interference, however tempting it may be to jump in and make any necessary readjustments. If we have built the plan correctly we will have included a set time for review, and it is important to stick to the schedule. If we are approached for assistance we should provide encouragement, and support or reward the effort that is being made to utilise the new ideas, but we should only offer reassurance and 'hands-off' support at this stage.

Evaluate and follow up

Having remained 'hands-off' for a period of time we can resume a more active role when we arrive at the evaluation and follow-up stage. We cannot overemphasise the importance of this final stage in the cycle.

It is appropriate here to make a link back to the sporting world where coaching plays such an important role in development. All successful sportspeople have a thorough review process. That is how they learn and improve. They look objectively at what went well, and what went badly. They then decide on the best course of action to improve their performance. In the workplace though we often see people who either ignore the things that go wrong and hope nobody notices, or blame their lack of success an external factor that they believe to be outside their control. If we are striving for a high-performance environment we have to eradicate such attitudes from our team. We need to build a strong and reliable review process to create a culture where people are happy to acknowledge the mistakes they make, learn from them, and become better as a result. The key is that we must make time for thorough evaluation before moving on. If we fail to do this then we may end up 'managing frustration'.

One of the things I remember learning in my physics lessons at school was that materials possess an 'elastic limit'. Simply put, this is a physical law which states that a material can be stretched and, providing its elastic limit is not exceeded, the material will return to its original shape. However if the elastic limit is exceeded, the new shape of the material will become permanent and non-reversible. Why is this relevant to performance management? Basically it is because people have very similar properties. Until our skills and abilities are stretched for long enough in a particular direction we will always return to our original 'shape'. Too many performance managers and coaches fail to recognise this. They spend valuable time developing new skills in people, but they don't evaluate and follow up well enough to ensure that the new skill is fully embedded as a habit before moving on. Upon returning to observe the same person in a similar situation in future they become frustrated when it appears that the individual has not learned from their previous coaching. The more times this is repeated the more frustrated the manager becomes with that member of the team, perhaps even to the point where they give up on the individual feeling that they are a lost cause. With better quality evaluation and follow-up it is possible to avoid getting stuck in a coaching cycle that leads to 'managing frustration'. If we use this stage effectively we can make any necessary readjustments to embed new skills in the right way. We should repeat this enough times to break the 'elastic limit' of the previous habit so that instead of reverting to the previous 'shape' a new habit is formed.

There are different opinions about how many repetitions are required to make, or break, a habit. Interestingly many of the theories seem to involve factors of seven. Perhaps this is something to do with the fact that a week has seven days, and that may give us seven opportunities, or multiples thereof, to build our new habit. I have heard many speakers on this topic refer to 7, 14, 21, or 28 times as the 'magic number'. Coming up with a specific number is not really as important as recognising that repetition is the key. The whole purpose of developing good habits is to ensure we remain in control, even when the pressure is on. We don't want to leave anything to chance, and therefore we should adopt a relentless approach to developing the right habits. In reality the amount of repetition may well be specific to the individual, or be dictated by the level of difficulty attached to the skill under development. The important thing is that we have enough resilience to stick to the task long enough so that eventually the new habit will be formed.

The next aspect of our follow-up is ongoing supervision. Getting the level of supervision right is a test of our performance management. It is vital that we demonstrate a clear understanding of both the topic for development, and the individual we are coaching. Appropriate supervision can be illustrated by describing what it feels like to compress and release a strong coil spring. Imagine we are squeezing a large spring between the palms of our hands, the more pressure we apply and the longer we hold it for, the more difficult it becomes. The force of the spring will cause us to tire until we can no longer hold it and we lose our grasp. At this point the spring will fly off unsupervised in any direction, and could end up anywhere, possibly causing damage to the obstacles it collides with en route. By releasing our grip more slowly we are able to control the force within the spring, use our energy more efficiently, and prevent any damage to the spring or the objects it might come into contact with once released. Supervising people in our team is very similar. If we supervise them too closely for long periods of time it will be both tiring for us and constraining for them. If we remove supervision too quickly, or with too little control, they could 'fly off' in the wrong direction with potentially damaging consequences. Applying the most appropriate level of supervision for each individual we are coaching will ensure that we provide enough freedom for them to develop without feeling constrained, as well as instilling confidence that we are there to support them whenever they need our help.

This illustration demonstrates that coaching is a fluid, continuous process. Having completed the cycle we should begin to move through the same cycle again, this time looking for new coaching opportunities that build on the development objectives we have already achieved.

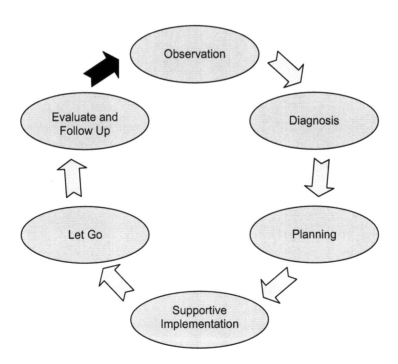

Getting organised and staying organised

Developing the right habits and using reliable 'models that work', will help us to get organised. Perhaps more importantly, we need a model that will help us to *stay* organised when the pressure is on.

Once we have defined the key activities that will deliver our business agenda it is important to remain focused on these, whilst at the same time, maintaining enough flexibility and agility to be able to respond to our ever-changing business priorities and the varying needs of our team. To achieve this, a dependable system of diary planning, prioritisation, and time management is required.

One approach is to employ a 'model week' to provide some structure. This will help us to be disciplined and remain on track with the most important things on our agenda so that they don't get crowded out by the more mundane distractions that bombard us every day. There are many people in management roles who don't use a model week – some are even openly opposed to the concept. This is possibly due to a perception that the model lacks flexibility. However if we are clear on the purpose of this technique, and how it should be used, we will not dismiss its relevance. The best way to illustrate this is by comparing the differences between a school timetable and a school curriculum. Our model week should not be built in the same way as a timetable – it should be constructed more like the curriculum. We cannot expect to build a model that precisely allocates our duties to the same time every day, or every week. Business life is just not that predictable. Taking a higher-level approach, as with a curriculum, we will identify the key themes of our business agenda which are to be developed during our working week to move performance forward. Whilst the themes may differ from business to business, it may help to consider the following generic components.

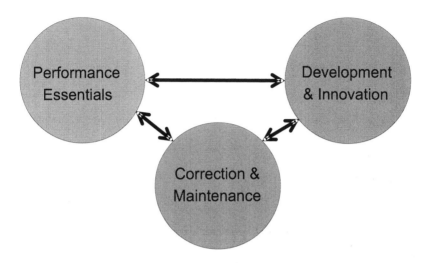

Once we are clear on our key themes, we can build a model week around them. We should be able to identify the specific activities that will influence all of our themes in the most efficient way possible. We can begin to schedule these activities into our diary, whilst allowing some flexibility in case we are faced with unexpected challenges. This process is, in itself, a challenge for many people. I have been approached, on numerous occasions, by individuals who want to develop better time management skills, asking for my view on how this can be achieved. However, as you may recall from an earlier example, before referring to a model, or a specific technique, these conversations always begin with a discussion about self-discipline.

A sales manager once told me that he knew he wasn't doing enough coaching with his team. "I need to manage my time better to do more coaching, but I'm too busy with all my emails and paperwork," he stated. In reply I asked, "If there was less work would more coaching get done? Have you got enough self-discipline to ensure that any time you might gain would be put to the best use?" The point is that we have to learn first how to diagnose our priorities so that we know we are working on the activities that will have the biggest impact on the performance we are driving for. Secondly, we must discipline ourselves to deliver those priorities without being distracted. Any additional workload and other commitments should always fit around the most important elements of our 'curriculum'. Looking towards time management skills in isolation as our solution could lead us to become very task-oriented, simply ticking off jobs on a 'to-do list', but not necessarily the right jobs in the right order. If we want to unlock precious time that we will allocate to important activities, like coaching for example, we should prioritise these in our model week – however we also need to develop the discipline required to deliver our priorities. Interestingly, we find that successful people always do precisely what needs to be done, when it needs doing. They don't make excuses for why they haven't had time to do all the important things. They don't need to – because they get the most important, or most valuable, things done first. They don't blame circumstances beyond their control because they take ownership and make things happen. It is a good idea to analyse how well we discipline ourselves to do the most important things, as dictated by our business agenda and our goal to create a high-performance environment. Achieving this level of success takes self-discipline, a skill we must learn if we want to make sense of performance management.

It is clear that getting organised involves much more than just developing time management techniques. It includes being in tune with the key themes that support our business agenda, deciding upon the most appropriate actions to develop those themes, organising them into a prioritised plan, and then sticking to our plan. We should challenge ourselves to see how we can maximise our efficiency by having the ability to progress as many of our key themes as possible using as few actions or tasks as possible. We highlighted earlier that an effective performance manager will group key activities together to find the 'single buttons that switch on several lights'. We must become adept at this, so it makes sense to train ourselves to develop all-encompassing actions that trigger multiple responses which generate a positive rate of return on the time we invest. We can illustrate how this works by going back to the earlier example involving the manager who approached me asking how he could find more time for coaching. To identify a solution for him we started to explore the opportunities that existed to build coaching into other activities. We identified a number of areas where it was possible for him to do this by structuring his time in a less transactional way, and introducing a more cultural style of management. Rather than attempting to do his transactional tasks more quickly to create additional time for coaching, he built his model week differently to include coaching within the important themes he identified. This enabled him to significantly increase the amount of coaching he conducted with his team because it became part of his everyday activities, rather than a separate transaction that he had to make time for. This approach changed the culture in the team, and their performance improved as a result. This underlines the point that cultural management is the most effective way to create an upward spiral in our team to accelerate our high-performance journey. Once this level of discipline becomes habitual we really start to see the benefit.

Early in my career I learned a sales tool that I later realised is effective as a model for performance management that gives us a structure to develop this high level of discipline. Anyone who has been involved in a sales role will recognise this to be a basic sales process model.

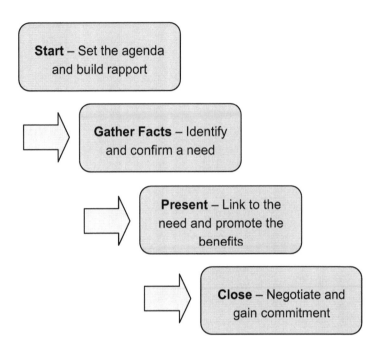

How is it possible to use a sales process model to help make sense of performance management, especially if we are not involved in managing sales? We would agree that a sales process is designed to motivate a customer to action – to purchase a product or a service. In much the same way, performance managers need to be able to motivate others to action. So it makes sense that this same model can be adapted for use in all of our formal performance management disciplines, such as one-to-ones, coaching, feedback, team meetings, and presentations, as well as in our more informal interactions. On each occasion we should start with an agenda, set the scene and build rapport. Next, we identify a need, before moving on to promote the benefits we expect to be gained from the session, and then finally asking for commitment to the actions which will achieve those benefits. Just like the sales process, we cannot expect success from the interactions we have with our team if we don't complete all the steps skilfully, and in the correct order. Also, by using this model to support our advance preparation we can link together a number of aspects under one agenda to 'press one button that switches on several lights'. For example, we may be planning a one-to-one to set objectives, but if we anticipate a coaching need we can prepare a role-play as part of the 'present' and 'close' stages to instil confidence, and obtain genuine commitment to the objectives.

I recall an example which demonstrates the value of learning how to use this model effectively. I observed a call-centre sales meeting where the manager was emphasising the need for all of his sales agents to answer more calls, selling them the benefit that the more calls they answered the more sales they would make. This was all well and good, but I envisaged a challenge coming from the agents around the fact that it was not possible for them *all* to speak to more customers because there was a finite number of calls coming into the centre, so essentially there wouldn't be enough to go around. This challenge was a very real possibility that could have put the team manager in an awkward position because he wasn't prepared for it. In effect he had employed the final two steps of the process by 'presenting the benefit' of taking more calls, and immediately expecting to 'gain commitment' from the team to do just that. A better way of handling this would have been to follow all four steps of the process. By 'setting the agenda and building rapport' the manager would be sure that his team were in the right frame of mind for the challenge he was about to present. During the 'gather facts and confirm need' section he could have highlighted to the team that more sales activity was needed and then facilitated a discussion to explore all the options available. The team may have come up with the solutions themselves. For example they may have suggested improving conversion, lengthening talk time to open up different sales opportunities, following up on previous leads, prospecting for new customers, and so on. The discussion would have enabled identification of a broader range of solutions. Rather than feeling that they were simply being told to answer more calls, each member of the team could select from a range of options that would deliver the aim of driving up productivity. The sales manager would have been able to make the link between the 'need' and the 'solutions' before asking for the team to 'commit' to the action plan. He would have retained control by preventing the risk of being challenged, and achieved a better outcome without controlling precisely what that outcome would be. Whilst this example involves a sales team, the same process is equally as effective as a model for any performance manager to gain commitment to action from their team, on either an individual or collective basis, whatever type of operation they are involved in.

Having explored some of the models that are most effective in shaping our habits, and instilling the level of discipline required to become more effective performance managers, we arrive finally at the most important one – the performance management framework. However, we will only cover this model very briefly in this section, because the entire book is dedicated to exploring and explaining how it works. It is worthwhile reminding ourselves at this point that this is a model which works equally well at different levels. So whilst the framework as explained throughout the book is designed to support our longer-term success, it is also a model that can be used in an everyday setting. However small a task may be, it remains our responsibility to set clear objectives that are linked to our business agenda, ensure appropriate training or refresher coaching is provided to maintain an environment that promotes a positive attitude to every task, and develop skills and abilities that become productive habits. The performance management framework is a model that can be used to good effect on both a small scale and a large scale, because if we follow this process we make it easier for our team to respond to our leadership.

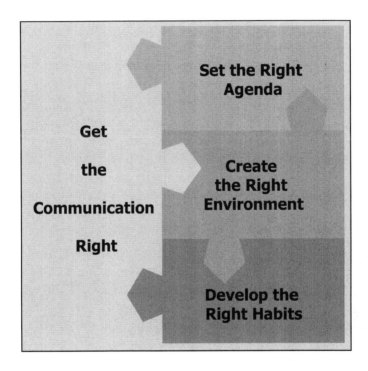

Developing a suite of models that we use consistently is pivotal to our success as a performance manager because these habits become the fabric of our leadership brand. As already acknowledged in an earlier section, our leadership brand sets the tone for our team. On that basis we must give strict consideration to the example we set.

Set a good example

As well as encouraging other people to develop habits that deliver high performance, we must set a good example by demonstrating these habits ourselves. It is fascinating to see how groups of people begin to emulate each other's behaviour as they spend more and more time together. We have already discovered that this feature of human interaction heavily influences our ability to create the right environment. Our responsibility deepens though when it comes to the development of habits within our team. 'Boss-watching' is something that happens in every team, and it will happen in ours whether we like it or not. Setting a good example is a really powerful way to drive behaviours and create habits. On the other hand, if we adopt a 'do as I say, not as I do' approach then we will struggle to produce a genuine high-performance culture. People are always watching, and they will take a lead from what they see. They will also be quick to excuse their own inadequacies if they observe a failing in their boss!

The importance of developing effective follow-up habits cannot be overemphasised. It is imperative that we set a good example of routine follow-up, and by doing so we benefit in a number of ways. To begin with we are able to confirm that our communication has been received and understood accurately and that no misconceptions have developed. We can check the status and progress of all the agreed actions that have been put in place to deliver our business objectives. Also, we will observe whether the habits we have coached into our team are developing in the right way. Another key benefit is that through regular follow-up we constantly reinforce in the minds of others the things that are important to us – so these are the things that will continue to receive greater focus. When people know that we are certain to follow up regularly they will develop stronger follow-up habits of their own which enhance their ability to deliver a superior performance without a high level of supervision. People will focus on what they perceive to be important. Achieving high performance involves us influencing this perception so that people respond by focusing more sharply on the standards we set for our team. Things we do, or say, infrequently are unlikely to be treated with high importance. On the other hand, the areas we refer to habitually will receive the required attention.

To show that we are serious about creating the right perception we should always set a good example when it comes to dealing with challenging issues that may arise in our team. Our reaction to these situations will always be closely scrutinised. For example, allowing inappropriate behaviour to go unchecked could be very damaging to the performance of our team because we create a perception that we are willing to tolerate low standards. This would expose us to a risk that everyone could begin to reduce their standards, even if they do so subconsciously. To prevent this from happening, we should always act swiftly and decisively when issues arise, even if this means adopting a 'zero tolerance' approach to inappropriate behaviour. It is important that we demonstrate to our team that we always act in harmony with the standards we set, which means we can never ignore issues however difficult they may be to deal with. We must be especially careful when it comes to those in our team who are high performers. We cannot make the mistake of trying to 'defend the indefensible'. Yes we should be proud of the successful people in our team, but not to the point where they can do no wrong in our eyes. Even if one of our top performers makes a mistake we should act in just the same way as we would for anyone else in the team. For instance, we shouldn't tolerate lateness, or extended breaks just because we know that a high performer will still hit their objectives. However good they are at exceeding their own target, it is unlikely they will be good enough to make up the shortfall of a whole team who begin to underperform because they don't like the fact that we have two sets of rules. If we are in the habit of treating every member of our team in a fair and consistent manner then the perception formed as a result of 'boss-watching' will be a positive one.

The way we handle pressure personally can also set a precedent in our team. A manager who worked for me once asked for 'a bit of slack' because he had so much going on in his private life. Obviously I was willing to offer my support through what was a difficult period for him personally. However, I gently reminded him that by approaching me to ask for the space he required, he had missed an extremely important point. Whilst it was appropriate that he ask my permission, in effect it wasn't me he needed to win the support of – it was his own team. If they didn't know that taking some time off, arriving late, and leaving early, was because of a temporary pressure in his personal life, they could have drawn the wrong conclusion – with potentially damaging consequences to the team performance. They may have perceived his behaviour to be a negative example, and responded by reducing their own effort instead of rallying round to deliver a more self-sufficient performance, which is what was necessary at that time. If this had happened, this manager would have exposed himself to more pressure at a time when he was ill-equipped to deal with it.

We also need to be aware of the reverse outcome and avoid behaving in a way that inadvertently puts more pressure on the people around us. I remember being told by a colleague about someone he had worked for in one of his previous roles who worked extremely long hours. Despite his assurance that he didn't expect his team to work in the same way, they still felt guilty that they didn't put in the same hours as their boss. When they left the office to go home to their families for some well deserved rest and relaxation they often felt bad about doing so. It sounded like a crazy situation to me, but it highlighted the point that it is important for us to set the right example in balancing our work responsibilities with our personal life. If we want people to be effective and perform well during work hours they have to 'switch off' and enjoy their personal time. We should make it clear that they will always be judged on what they deliver in the time they spend at work, not on the length of time they spend there. This approach enhances productivity, but to secure this benefit we should set a good example ourselves in the way we balance our work life and personal life.

It is this balance that will also help us to find more enjoyment when we are at work. We spend a lot of time in the workplace so it helps if we enjoy it. If we are in the habit of looking for ways we can enjoy our role, then those around us will do the same. Enjoyment includes celebrating the small successes along the way to our big achievements. If we look for enjoyment, even in everyday tasks, we will contribute higher energy and greater enthusiasm to our interactions with others. This will help us to develop more productive relationships within our team. Relaxed and happy people are far more likely to achieve great results for the team because they will contribute more liberally and exhibit greater creativity, which enhances the multiplier effect. Setting the right example personally will have a positive impact on our high-performance culture.

It is fitting that *Develop the Right Habits* is the final section of the performance management framework to be covered. Whilst it is communication that links all of the sections of our framework together, it is our habits that enable our success as a performance manager to stand the test of time. We could set the right agenda once, and create the right environment once – but developing the right habits means we can repeat these actions to deliver consistently high performance over and over again. Reliable habits will not make us perfect — but they will help us to get our performance management right most of the time.

$$6$$

Getting it Right Most of the Time

Putting it all together

Now that we have explored the key areas of the performance management framework we can consider how we will put it all together.

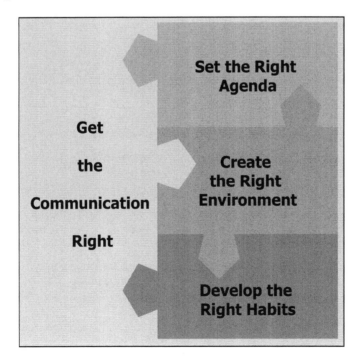

We should begin by setting a realistic personal development plan for ourselves to address the aspects of the framework where we feel there is room for improvement. None of us can expect to be the perfect performance manager. We will not get everything right all of the time – but we must challenge ourselves to get most of it right, most of the time. In reality our team will never demand perfection from us. However they will expect consistency – and they deserve as much. Ironically, managing people is very often an inconsistent business, but if we consistently reach high performance standards in the way we manage people they will be more likely to deliver a consistently high performance in return. By setting consistent standards we can expect consistent results.

This begins with the way we communicate with our team. Communication is at the core of all the tools and skills related to performance management. It is crucial to our ultimate success, as the way we communicate links all the other elements of our framework together. It holds the key to developing productive relationships within our own team and with our stakeholders. We must learn how to manage the impact of our communication and understand the reaction we get from others around us. The people in our team should always know precisely what is required of them, and how we expect them to deliver their objectives. They need to receive regular constructive feedback on how effectively they are contributing towards the team goals, and we need regular feedback too so that we can keep our 'finger on the pulse' and stay in control of the business agenda without being controlling.

Establishing our team culture on these terms will contribute to an environment that is conducive to delivering successful outcomes. Within this environment we will be able to nurture our team brand and develop a set of values that everyone in the team accepts and lives by. This brand should be something that everyone wants to belong to, and is a catalyst for the multiplier effect which becomes a powerful force that will contribute significantly to our journey towards high performance.

Creating a high-performing team culture involves investing in people, giving them a sense of pride, and continually developing them so that they are capable of delivering bigger and better results. By cultivating a desire for continuous improvement, and establishing a robust coaching programme for our team, we will create an upward spiral that delivers a superior performance across all aspects of our business scorecard.

Giving individuals a free licence to be themselves will profit our team culture further because they will become more enthusiastic about shaping the business that they belong to. By contributing ideas, offering constructive feedback and making suggestions, they become more engaged in our shared vision, and they take more pride in being a valued member of the team.

Throughout all of this we must remember that our leadership style is based on our own values and beliefs, so we should always be true to who we are. Our team need to see our business focus, our passion for success, and our enthusiasm for delivering great results, against the backdrop of our own unique personality. Seeing that we can enjoy ourselves and that we have the ability to lead them with a genuine smile on our face, will contribute to their enjoyment of belonging to a high-performing team. They will continue to invest their focus, passion, enthusiasm, and energy, into driving our performance spiral upwards. When we see these positive behaviours we should acknowledge them and, where appropriate, reward them too so that everyone can take satisfaction from the results delivered through the combined efforts of the team. It is essential that we celebrate every one of our successes along this journey, however small they are, to demonstrate *our* pride in *their* achievements.

Habits that drive continuous success

We want our status as a high-performing team to last. We will accomplish this by assembling the component parts of our success formula into habitual routines, and by developing similar productive habits into every individual member of our team. This is a constant challenge and we will never be able to say that we have completed this aspect of performance management. Knowing this, it makes sense to develop the habit of reminding our team, and reminding them again, following up as many times as is necessary to develop and reinforce winning habits. We can achieve this by building a suite of models that we are confident will work over, and over, again to bring us success every time we repeat the action.

As we said at the outset, there is no quick fix. A high-performance culture cannot be created overnight – although we can begin our journey towards high performance immediately by applying the principles of the performance management framework. In conjunction with our own skills and abilities, as well as a strong desire for success, this framework will help us to get the best out of our own leadership style and the best out of the people we lead. By putting it all together and striving to get most of it right most of the time, we will achieve success and enjoy the privilege of leading a high-performing team.

Making sense of performance management involves making sense to the people we work with. We may become a great performance manager, but we could never achieve this without the great people we have around us. When they deliver outstanding results we must always remember to give them the credit they deserve for the performance they deliver. We should never forget that *they* are the most important component of any equation that results in our success, and we should thank them for giving us the opportunity to be the best performance manager we can be.

Index